White People and Black Lives Matter

Johanna C. Luttrell

White People and Black Lives Matter

Ignorance, Empathy, and Justice

Johanna C. Luttrell
University of Houston
Houston, TX, USA

ISBN 978-3-030-22491-2   ISBN 978-3-030-22489-9   (eBook)
https://doi.org/10.1007/978-3-030-22489-9

Cover illustration: roberuto / Getty Images
Cover design: Tom Howey

This Palgrave Macmillan imprint is published by the registered company Springer Nature Switzerland AG
The registered company address is: Gewerbestrasse 11, 6330 Cham, Switzerland

PREFACE

This book interrogates white responses to black-led movements for racial justice. Such responses are sites of clarity regarding white identity, because whiteness shows itself not only in white people's self-regarding feelings but more so in dialogic responses to public, democratic social movements and discourse. Yet, my purpose here is not to define whiteness for its own sake but to clear the weeds of white people's obstacles to respecting black-led social movements like Black Lives Matter (BLM). I probe reactions which often prevent white people from, according to black activists, the full range of human emotion and expression, including joy, anger, mourning, and political action.

My ultimate objective is not to indicate the ways in which white people might be racist and so deserve moral condemnation. Even though a white public's responses to black-led social movements can indeed be racist, such an approach that merely dwells upon the state of white people's souls is unhelpful to the aims of the social movements in the first place. Instead, the aim is constructive: a philosophical self-reflection on the ways in which 'white' reactions to BLM stand in the way of the movement's important work. The hope is that coming to terms with our own reactions is a step toward cultivating better ones, responses that acknowledge human dignity, and the richness of varied forms of human expression. As such, the book's aim is not to interpret BLM. That work is being done by scholars and activists whose positionality and commitment allow them insight which, as a white author, I do not and need not, possess.[1]

Again, this work is an attempt to understand whiteness communally and individually, as seen phenomenologically in white responses to black-led social movements. It promotes white self-reflection for the purposes of political solidarity. That said, qua capacity in my own raced self, I have been trained over a lifetime not to "see" whiteness, its origins, effects, or agents. James Baldwin writes that white people in the United States "are, in effect, still trapped in a history which they do not understand; and until they understand it, they cannot be released from it."[2] Baldwin describes myself as much as anyone. Many of my advantages have come from my training in *not* seeing whiteness. As I discuss in Chap. 1, efforts as self-reflection are notoriously shoddy; they too often end up in defensiveness and idealization, rather than honesty. Many non-white critical philosophers of race, popular writers, and activists write accurately about whiteness because they are, in a very original sense, more objective: They are gazing outward, toward another, rather than attempting to gaze inward.[3]

Yet knowledge and ignorance are not simple. The ways in which I do and do not know whiteness are complex tracings of conscious and unconscious play of ignorance and awareness. It is possible that this kind of knowledge is akin to the way Plato speaks about learning, as *anamnesis*—a remembering of what has been forgotten.[4] Whiteness could in this sense be a process of un-learning, a mandated forgetting. Power and interests promote forgetting and make certain processes; in this case, the construction of whiteness, invisible to certain people, and hyper-visible to others. In a society structured by white supremacy, white people's power depends on forgetting and people of color's survival depends upon remembering. Writing, then, can be a form of learning, in the Platonic sense of excavation. That is, the act of writing itself can be a way of trying to understand, remembering what one is encouraged to forget, because it is an active participation in knowledge's construction. Regarding discussions on racial justice and social movements, I have felt the need to do more than just be a consumer of other people's observations; I have found myself needing to participate in knowledge's construction. I wrote this book because I think it is important that white people in the United States respect BLM, and I address some of their objections philosophically. I did not write this book because, either in my capacity as a philosopher or a white person, I am more an expert on the topic than people of color whose survival depends, in many ways, on their perceptivity to whiteness.

In the process of writing, I would like to thank the interdisciplinary faculty reading group at University of Houston for their early, very helpful comments, especially Rachel Afi Quinn and Eesha Pandit; the Political

Theory reading group at the University of Houston; the participants of the 2017 California Roundtable on the Philosophy of Race group for their thorough feedback; Ronald Sundstrom for his early comments on a chapter's working draft; Naomi Zack for her feedback and encouragement; my colleagues at the Hobby School of Public Affairs for the academic freedom and initiative they inspire. Thanks to Thibaud, who gave me confidence that this book was possible and who allowed me to finish the book while he took care of our new baby. This book is dedicated to the activists in Houston, Texas, who taught me so much about social commitment, radical love, and the revolutionary South. May the book be in some small way a help, or at least not a hindrance, to your work. I am grateful for my readers, support system, and activist community; any distortions or misrepresentations are entirely my own.

Houston, TX   Johanna C. Luttrell

NOTES

1. In philosophy of race, see, for instance, Christopher Lebron, *The Making of Black Lives Matter: A Brief History of an Idea* (Oxford: Oxford UP, 2017); Naomi Zack, *White Privilege and Black Rights: The Injustice of US Police Racial Profiling and Homicide* (NY: Rowman and Littlefield, 2015). In African-American studies, see, for instance, Keeanga-Yahmatta Taylor, *From #BlackLivesMatter to Black Liberation* (Chicago: Haymarket, 2016) In History, Barbara Ramsey, *Making All Black Lives Matter: Reimagining Freedom in the Twenty-First Century* (Oakland: University of California Press, 2018) In political science, Juliet Hooker, "Black Lives Matter and the Paradoxes of Black Politics: From Democratic Sacrifice to Democratic Repair", *Political Theory* 44, no.4 (2016): 448–469.
2. James Baldwin, *The Fire Next Time* (New York: Vintage, 1993), 8.
3. In philosophy, see, for instance, George Yancy, What White Looks Like: African-American Philosophers on the Whiteness Question (New York: Routledge, 2004) and Linda Martín Alcoff, *The Future of Whiteness* (Cambridge: Polity, 2015).
4. Plato, *Phaedo*, trans. G.M.A. Gruebe (New York: Hackett, 1977), 26.

CONTENTS

CHAPTER 1

Getting My People

1.1 Whiteness and Self-Reflection

Many of us white people want to claim some degree of empathy, if not solidarity, with the noble aims of Black Lives Matter, that is, dignity and justice for black people. But before we can claim the virtue that comes with either empathy or solidarity, we first need some humility about what we already know and to engage in some self-reflection about the ways in which whiteness, as a political project, arrests the veracity of our knowledge claims and obscures our vision on the matter. Even the very claim to virtuous empathy or solidarity itself works to conceal its own deficiency. There is a constraint on what white people know about black-led political movements for racial justice, a ceiling to what a white imaginary hears in a black political speech. Given that constraint, it is incumbent upon us to linger for a while not only on the content of our truth claims about movements like BLM but their limits. Coming to terms with the boundaries of those limits, the mechanisms by which their frontiers are drawn and re-drawn, is a process of coming to terms with ourselves as white people. Black political speech is not unintelligible, it is just that our confidence about what we *already know* halts any deeper process of understanding in its tracks. Whiteness structures many of our assumed worldviews and creates its own acknowledged set of truths, its own world of common sense. When pressed, our comfortable, passive axioms about black-led movements can reveal themselves not self-evident truths but as engines of power and interests that fuel a political project of anti-blackness. In other words,

© The Author(s) 2019
J. C. Luttrell, *White People and Black Lives Matter*,
https://doi.org/10.1007/978-3-030-22489-9_1

if we want to have a chance at a just engagement, belief, empathy, or solidarity with BLM, we need first to understand the limits of a white epistemology of black political movements and the ways in which whiteness
emerges against liberatory movements.

Self-reflection is difficult. The Delphic Oracle's command "know thy-
self" is probably more aspirational than feasible, at least for mortals. The
worry about self-knowledge's slim chances still presents itself in modernity. In Shakespeare's *King Lear*, for instance, Lear's daughters lament of
their father "he hath ere but slenderly known himself".[1] Lear was never
able to face the ravages he enacted upon his family, to face the kind of man
he was. He could only ever achieve fleeting moments of self-recognition,
not enough to survive or to treat his daughters justly. He rebuffed attempts
to show himself, to himself.

There are structural and personal obstacles to self-reflection. I might
not want to attempt it, because sometimes when I catch glimpses of
myself, I see things I would rather not. In general, I like surrounding
myself with people who would not show my failures to me, and I might
sacrifice even honest respect for risking that kind of vulnerability. Such is
the function of defensiveness. Accurate mirrors are uncomfortable and
painful, and I generally prefer sacrificing light for warmth. In many
instances, I do not have to live in a kind of culture that would encourage
an honest self-accounting, so to cover over un-comfortability, I tend to
substitute self-praise for self-appraisal, naval gazing for reckoning.

People of color in the United States do at times try to show white
people to ourselves, and they, like Cordelia to Lear, are most often
rebuffed. We—from here on, by "we", I mean white people in the United
States, this author included—mostly do not want to hear it, even if we say
we do. We do not want to look in that particular mirror, and we must not
have our survival tethered to it.

One historical and paradigmatic example: Journalist and activist Ida
Wells-Barnett led a Reconstruction-era campaign to uncover the systemic
racist and gendered logic that undergirded lynching in the United States.
Her campaign was more successful in England than in the States, where the
public was not forced to look at itself.[2] The reception in the States, as Wells
recounts, was at first met with defensiveness and not only defensiveness
from where one might expect, i.e., from southern white men. It was northern white women's temperance leagues who fielded vehement and under-
handed resistance to her campaign. These women were what in modern
parlance we call might call self-identified "allies" or what Janine Jones

might call "goodwill whites": those who have a self-professed commitment to black civil rights and believe in racial equality.[3] In other words, they were the progressives of their time. They supported emancipation. One Mrs. Williard, who called herself a "friend and well-wisher" to Wells' movement, was upset that Wells implicated white women in the violence of southern white men. Wells herself gave an honest account of white women's voluntary and consensual relationships with black men, their subsequent denial of these relationships, and their final complicity in the lynching of their love interests at the hands of "chivalrous" white male protectors. In response, New Englander women defended the southerners on the grounds of white virtue and Christian hospitality, yoking their own identities with their southern counterparts, and outsourcing cruelties as exceptional events inflicted by lower-class whites, not the upstanding Christian citizens they themselves knew. There was no recognition that northern women also held and supported the symbolic logic of lynching, in terms of their belief in the stereotypes of the widespread criminalization of black men and the over-sexualizing of black women. These so-called facts about Reconstruction's former slaves operated with the same intuitive conviction of veracity in the North as in the South. Thus, any honest look at lynching as systemic and not accidental would incur an opportunity for self-reflection, and that was not an opportunity either northern or southern whites—women or men—were willing, for the most part, to take up.

In our current era, what should be called the Black Lives Matter era, the first moment of rebuff comes when we beg off the name that people of color give to us: white. We will not see ourselves in the confines of that specific moniker. What does it mean, we ask ourselves, to be white? It does not sound like anything good. Is it an insult? An ontological status? A neutral descriptor? (unlikely).[4] We chafe at being called white because it sounds like we are being called a dirty name, and in truth sometimes we are. But what would it mean to take up that name, as soiled as it reads? To call oneself white sounds like it would mean admitting to a nebulous guilt, everywhere and nowhere, and therefore a guilt that cannot be real. The word "privileged" reads similarly: a politically correct label meant to implicate me in something to which I did not consent. And regardless, I am innocent. I did nothing to you, personally. My own parents were relatively poor and worked hard, I have worked hard for what I have, and slavery has been over for a long time. Besides, some of you have more wealth than me, and those who have less have pathological families, nothing like my own. Admitting to being white sounds like an admission of guilt, and that is unfair.

Besides, people who think that whiteness is a *thing*, a category with defi-nite meaning, are white supremacists. I share nothing with them, they are the guilty ones, and moreover they are exceptions and not the rule. The intellectual position here is that taking on whiteness as an ontological status gives it too much credence and affirms race' existence as a real entity. Specifically, this position holds that affirming racial "reality" means standing against Martin Luther King's understood mandate, widely assumed to be the entire inheritance of the Civil Rights Movement, that one should judge people by the content of their character alone.[5] I want to distance myself from the Klan and the [lower-class] southerners, the real racists, because not all white people are the same. There is no "we" here. When black people talk about white people as a group, it irks me, because, on the one hand, it lumps everyone together. On the other hand, it assumes that I did not have hardship in my own life to overcome. Thus, I will not be named by you.

Such is, in Aristotelean terms, the *doxa*, the common position that frames the first reaction of a white public upon feeling the weight of a directed description.[6] In Aristotle, *doxa* shows up as intuitive truths, widely held reactions that appear on the scene as "common sense" and as such they carry no apparent burden of justification. But they are not yet reasonable or sensible. Aristotle's philosophical method was to push on and uncover these *doxic* belief systems, until they revealed internal contradictions. The internal contradictions produced a tension in the form of an *aporeia*, a tricky point of a seemingly inextricable knot. Unraveling the knot was the beginning and the work of philosophy. The conviction that white people are not them-selves raced and the determination that acts of cruelty toward black people are exceptions and not the rule are examples of *doxa*. To many white people, they appear on the scene as self-evident common sense, so true that they are intuitions that do not need explicit justifications. Yet, they contain intermi-nable contradictions, needing to be philosophically unraveled.

What holds us back from reflection on our own doxa, from unraveling its contradictions? For one, we are not practiced in self-reflection, because we have not needed it for our survival. The mirror of self-reflection between white people and people of color in the United States is, cru-cially, asymmetrical. White people can rebuff the feedback they receive from black populations, but black people cannot do the same. Ijeoma Oluo writes that, as a black woman living in ostensibly progressive Seattle, she must understand how white culture operates because it is essential for her survival. She has been entrenched in whiteness her entire life, operat-ing within the [white] American dream. She understands how structural racism works, because she needs to understand. She has also needed the knowledge of what white people think of black people, because she reasonably perceives her own survival is tethered to their mirror. She writes of growing up, "I had to learn how to not get suspended by white teachers, how to not get arrested by white cops, how to not get fired by white supervisors."[7] However, Oluo emphasizes, white people do not have, or need to have, a similar, deep knowledge of black people, or, for that matter, their own whiteness. "Your [white people's] survival has never depended on your knowledge of white culture. In fact, it's required your ignorance. *The dominant culture does not have to see itself to survive because culture will shift to fit its needs.*"[8] Power has the luxury of denying itself self-reflection, as long as it stays in power. Power can maintain itself through shifting formations of self-delusion and outright lies, while doing so can deny the baseness of its tactics.[9]

I do not know if we can be self-reflective enough to be empathetic. Are the obstacles to reflection interminable, the limits too entrenched? The current landscape could be read that way. In *Citizen*, her work of collected poems, Claudia Rankine lists some of the names of black people who have been murdered by police in the United States, since 2011. The names come one after another and then fade out. After the faded names, she writes: "because white men can't/police their imagination/black people are dying."[10] In *The Condition of Black Lives is one of Mourning*, Rankine writes that, because children are being killed because they are black, "Our mourning, this mourning, is in time with our lives. There is no life outside of our reality here. Is this something that can be seen and known by parents of white children? This is the question that nags me."[11] Rankine's question—whether white parents of white children can see and know the mourning of black parents for their children—motivates this chapter too,[12] and really, is the motivating inquiry of the book.

The question could be framed differently: If white people *can* understand, *will* they? Of course, there's the Kantian insight here: ability is a necessary precondition for willing, as *should* implies *can*. But action's relation to knowledge and ignorance is a complex, ever-shifting map of interactions between ability and will. The following chapters show it is indeed possible for white people to empathize with black experience, in imperfect and limited ways that do not presume absolute compatibility but are nevertheless *enough* to motivate democratic actions in solidarity. Thus, if the question of ability becomes to some degree settled, the question of will becomes more urgent.

Ignorance works, in one sense, by maintaining an ambivalence between intentional dismissal and quasi-unintentional self-delusion.[13] This ambiguity, the back and forth, is undoubtedly irrational. It is more a matter of the deep psychological contradiction rather than ordered philosophical arguments, and so there is a limit to how philosophy can address these contradictions besides attempts at merely drawing them out of concealment. The actual work of unravelling of such psychologies is done in relationships.

Certainly, white people want to claim they understand and empathize with black experience. It is important to our self-conception that we can and do possess empathy. But we get ahead of ourselves. Janine Jones stresses that empathy cannot be claimed before belief. That is, before we can claim the virtue of empathy, we must first *believe* the experiences of black people. I would add that the public demonstrations with movements like BLM present ample opportunities for such belief, moments where we could afford epistemic credibility. We meet those moments, though, with disbelief, paired with a reassurance that we are empathetic. Whites first must pay attention to such movements—to listen, then permit belief— before we can call ourselves empathetic. Jones stresses that she is not interested in investigating the white person who means to harm blacks, who may indeed possess empathetic understanding, but the kind of understanding "which Iago possessed with respect to Othello".[14] Rather, she is interested in the person who does not want to or simply cannot believe that harm is being done in relation to race. This person is a "goodwill white", perhaps a white liberal who admires the gains of the civil rights movement and publicly decries racism. To be sure, I think Jones' description of "goodwill whites" describes most people, or at least the public *doxa*, the deeply held, half conscious and half-unconscious beliefs that constitute the confines of public debate in the United States. She is not only describing people on the left of the political spectrum. Who, really, believes themselves to be consciously wishing harm to another on the basis of their race? Even the white supremacist of the Charlottesville marches would not describe themselves this way.[15]

Jones writes that Thomas Jefferson is "the moral father" of goodwill whites, the founder who simultaneously believed in the idea of life, liberty, and the pursuit of happiness and at the same time could not "empathize with the plight of a slave mother whose child was sold", who could "not *see* that black slave women had hearts with feelings too, feelings of their children".[16] Jefferson's is the essential, and frustrating, internal tension goodwill whites hold, this mismatch between ideal justice and non-ideal reality.[17] Jones writes: "Goodwill whites want to be *or are seen as being* (perhaps especially in their own eyes) champions of liberty, much as they perceive their founding fathers to have been."[18] However, like Jefferson, "goodwill whites ... attempt to avoid discussions of racism ... because, like their ideological father, they seek to avoid confrontation and friction, especially of an internal nature."[19] As Jones describes, Jefferson's ideological descendants, are first unwilling or unable to say, or perhaps believe, that they are white. Other people are "raced", we are not. Because we are unable or unwilling to understand our own situation, we do not achieve empathy. Jones locates this failure of empathy not as much in ability as motivation. A white observer might not think it is worth their time to construct an analogous map to black people's experience, even though they could. "His [the white observer's] belief would indicate to him that is it beside the point to look for or construct such an experience."[20] Jones hits on something important here. If whites can indeed empathize, they must first believe that such an effort is worth their time and attention. This question of what is "worth one's time" is the sticking point. The limits to the white episteme, then, are not so much a matter of truth as priorities, or rather, priorities masked as truth. The white political project appears on the scene as a problem of belief, but its engine is preference. A choice draws the boundary of understanding, a choice about which direction to turn my head, my attention, toward whom, for how long.

Within this asymmetric dialectic where understanding flows one direction (blacks to white, people of color to whiteness) but not the other (white to black, whiteness to people of color), black-led social movements like Black Lives Matter (BLM) carve out a space for black voices and black dignity in an environment that affords neither. This democratic social movement breaks from the definitions white populations give to people of color and then concurrently demand that the white majority see black populations in the light of their own positive self-definitions. In doing so, they demand a reckoning of our—white people's—own self-image. The white majority can, as I will describe more in Chap. 3, rebuff such movements in many ingenious ways.

Thus, many African-American writers have expressed exhaustion over trying to defend black-led social movements to an audience of white people, to the detriment of building and sustaining themselves and their own communities. Concurrently, the liberal white doxa is that white people are willing to listen while people of color do the work to untangle white supremacy. But this "listening", another possible claim to white virtue, is an expectation that others will *do for*, and it can show up as a demand. It is the sort of voyeurism I address in Chap. 3, which demands vulnerability from one party—the BLM writers and activists—while remaining invulnerable oneself. There is a certain kind of emotional harm upon being and body of the one to whom this asymmetrical demand is addressed. Listening, is, of course, the first step to empathy, but white listeners often impose a series of expectations in a performance of black grievance as part of a willingness to "listen", and these expectations are a burden.[21]

For instance, Christopher Lebron writes of the harm of the white imagination upon black people and black people's response. Lebron expresses that in order to give compassion to himself, and to live in the space of self-respect where he wants to live, he cannot constantly see himself through white people's imagination or constantly tackle those imaginings.[22] Doing so would risk splitting his own consciousness. Lebron explains that his notion of radical self-regard draws from Zora Neale Hurston's. Hurston described becoming frustrated that the white literary audience failed to appreciate Janie, the character in her 1930s novel *Their Eyes Were Watching God*. By the end of the book, Janie ends up economically and spiritually liberated. The white response at the time expected Janie to be oppressed, without celebration or joy. Lebron explains, "When Hurston writes of her irritation that whites constantly expect her narrative to be sorrowful, she is bristling in the attempt to truncate the range of her human interests and emotions. Her white interlocutors fail to realize that perhaps Hurston is more invested in moments of joy rather than melancholy."[23] Lebron, in tradition of Hurston, is making space to dwell in the full range of human emotions and so to be fully human. Here he is speaking of the pressure put to conform to respectability politics, as present in philosophical scholarship, the pressure to keep white expectations of black people intact, including the expectation that the range of human emotions be cauterized, while black people are doing [impossible] work to measure up to them.

Thus, Lebron writes that it is impossible for him to write for two audiences—one he calls the "morally dim-witted" and the other he calls the less dim-witted, but much more self-satisfied, white liberal. To note, Lebron's categories of non-empathetic white people correspond to Jones' categories of the Iago-inspired group vs. the goodwill whites. The morally dim-witted are those for whom, for Lebron, one must *argue* at all that black people have dignity in the first place.

To be morally dim-witted is to be a person convinced of the justice of his or her position yet whose moral perceptions are so deeply mired in racial privilege that the critical perception and judgement needed to correctly interpret problems is suppressed to the point of motivating asinine observations and assertions. The harshness of that statement does nothing to mitigate its truth. Imagine what it is like to read, as a black person, in the wake of Freddie Gray nearly losing his head—literally—while in police custody: well, if he wasn't doing anything wrong, why did he run? As if being legitimately afraid of the police, in a city where the "Nickel Ride" is a widely known institution of police abuse, were reason at all to be practically decapitated by the state. Or, more recently with reference to Sandra Bland: why was she acting to arrogantly with the officer by refusing to put out her cigarette? As if asking, with the strong voice of a citizen, why one is being badgered is reason at all to be slammed face first on the ground.[24]

Lebron here references Freddie Gray, a man killed in Baltimore, after police broke his neck in the back of a police wagon. He also mentions Sandra Bland, a woman in Waller County, Texas, who was pulled over for failing to signal a lane change and then three days later found dead in her jail cell. For Lebron, there is no point in *arguing* with a person who cannot be persuaded that it is reasonable to feel scared of the police based on repeated personal and communal experience or that one deserves death for reasonably asserting one's dignity. The matter is one of epistemic justice: If I do not believe a person about their own experience or feelings, we have no common plane to continue a discussion.[25] Logic, reason, and argument, much less empathy, cannot begin.

Nevertheless, for Lebron, while the morally dim-witted are bad news, white liberals can be more harmful. In contrast to Jones' claim that goodwill whites do lack the motivation to believe black experience, Lebron claims that white liberals for the most part do in fact believe the experiences and feelings of many POC in the United States. However, they take only self-satisfaction in the fact of their belief, without concurrent action or risk. "[White liberals] ... can in fact be more troubling precisely because their self-reflection often extends as far as their sense of righteousness is near their hearts, which often turns out to be quite near. These people do not want me to live well—the morally dim-witted are unconcerned with my well-being; the self-satisfied are unmotivated to do much to help improve it."[26] Both Jones and Lebron consider motivation to be the crucial sticking point, but motivation occurs at different points in the process. For Jones, the lack of motivation is most salient at the point of belief. For Lebron, the lack of motivation comes at the point of action.

I was present at some of the protests and vigils to honor Sandra Bland, in Waller County and around Houston, Texas, in 2015. At that time, I was beginning to understand how on point the consternation and dismay was directed at liberal well-wishers and self-described allies. After Bland's death in July, activists including Brandi Holmes, Fran Watson, and Rev. Hannah Bonner, camped outside the Waller County jail with signs, questioning each person who came and went, reminding them what happened on the premises, demanding change. The activists' commitment was evident by anyone familiar with a Houston summer, anyone who has felt how hot 100-plus-degree day at full humidity can be. No one goes outside unless they have to, let alone spends all day in the sun. I put off going myself—it was too hot, I was not ready to be that uncomfortable. That summer and fall, activists worked to expose entrenched racism in the police force and jailers and pushed for bail reform, greater transparency, and independent oversight. The protest and vigils expressed all ranges of emotions, from celebration and honor of Bland's life and ambitions, exuberance at increasing collective power, to mourning, grief, frustration, and anger.[27] But when I spoke with many of my white university colleagues, people who articulated shock and condemnation for Bland's treatment, they were more than willing to have intellectual debates about matters like police videos, but not at all willing to change their routine/agenda to have face-to-face encounters with the activists. After a while, I got the sense that although it is hard work for activists to prepare themselves to encounter daily acts of resistance with a rural, racist police force, those confrontations might not inspire the kind of everyday exhaustion of encounters with people like myself: people who come up in urban, educated, white, liberal immovability.

My white milieu conveyed a sort of passive whiteness, a passivity which in practice turned out to be anti-blackness. In our contentment and self-satisfaction in positioning ourselves as observers, rather than opening to the vulnerability it would take to try and participate, I and my white colleagues and friends did not advance BLM. A counterfactual thought experiment: I try to imagine if a broad swath of academics from the University of Houston had organized a caravan an hour outside of town to stand behind the BLM activists outside of the Waller County Jail in the wake of Bland's death. What if University of Houston students had caravanned themselves out to Prairie View A & M University, the historically black college where Bland had just started her job, to march in solidarity for visit to town hall meetings on the subject? Instead, our passivity—appearing as allyship, justified as virtue—foreclosed these possibilities for solidarity.

For critical race theorists and activists, that passive whiteness would manifest itself as anti-blackness is unsurprising and indicative of the way whiteness, and white supremacy, works on a large scale. Ayan Adbulle writes that "Whiteness is centered by Blackness … anti-Blackness anchors Whiteness."[28] In reflecting on the creation of the first exhibition of the Racial Imaginary Institute, Claudia Rankine reflects that the curators had long discussions about how to represent whiteness artistically, in a way that does not further reify or admire whiteness, or, as Monica Youn explained, "without centering white experience while relegating others to the margins?"[29] The institute settled on representing whiteness through anti-black violence. That move is not, I would argue, accidental. It is ensconced in histories white people do not see: the histories of colonialism that, according to Frantz Fanon and Sara Ahmed, make up our bodies, our comportment, our way of being-in-the-world.[30] The colonial histories trace themselves, invisibly [to many white people], through the legacy of slavery, convict leasing, Jim Crow, mass incarceration to dogged color-blindness and claims of post-racialism.[31] The last two stages—the assumed demand to colorblindness and post-racialism—work to mask, as colonialism masked its own brutalities, the connection between whiteness and anti-blackness. Activists attempt to uncover these histories, but the kind of white ignorance that conceals these stories is the kind that, as Mills phrases, "fights back". Rankine contends: "the not-knowing on the part of whiteness is an active investment in not wanting to know."[32]

However, I am going to object to someone naming whiteness as part of my identity and implying that I am sullied by anti-blackness and the colonial histories I myself have not lived. Are you saying I am a bad person? If such a claim were leveled at me, I might take it as an insult if I were conservative, or, if I were liberal, I might accept it and do nothing besides insisting that everyone feels bad about it. Either of those responses, though, misunderstands the nature of the claim. No one is accusing me of "sin", in the sense of a motionless certainty about my being, as if anti-blackness was stagnant water pooling inside of me. If anti-black practices were "sins" in the ecclesiastical sense, my liberal, white guilt would be rightly subject to Thomas Chatterton Williams' critique. Williams wonders if there has ever "been another group that willingly castigates itself over its own presumed racial essence the way woke whites are increasingly incentivized to hate on themselves?"[33] That kind of white self-flagellation is fruitless and tiresome. It only works to signal "in-group" affinities between other [self-described] "woke" white folks. Rather than a sin, passive whiteness should be understood in the Aristotelean sense of a habit. Aristotle theorizes habits, the practices that make up virtues and vices, as activities, ways of being at work. They are dynamic, living, and growing things, capable of being cultivated, in adulthood, into meaningful action. So, if I agree that passive whiteness turns out to be anti-blackness, what I might do about that is to reflect on my own and my group habits that reinforce such passivity and then work to change those habits so that I can claim the solidarity with black-led social movements to which my self-described allyship aspires. I might make myself vulnerable to risk encounters with BLM activists, rather than form educated opinions about the movement from the sidelines.

Given passive whiteness' anti-blackness, Lebron reflects that when he tries to write with these two audiences in mind, the liberal well-wishers, on one hand, and the morally dim-witted, on the other, it tends up being some of his worst writing—it is not as honest as he needs it to be nor is it effective in terms of his own liberation. "When I write at my best, I am not writing to you—I am writing to me for you. I'm sorry, but I'm too busy with the struggle to be much concerned with whether you agree with me."[34] Lebron stresses that his most honest and liberatory writing is one where he is constructing a space for himself where he can stand in dignity, autonomy, and respect, and the writing is giving that to himself.

Susana Morris takes the matter a step further. Instead of requesting that scholars and activists of color once again address white people's prejudice, she exhorts white scholars to "get your people", to take up the mantle of undoing one's own white communities' racist responses that distort democracy and threaten the dignity of brown and black people in the United States.[35] As a queer, black woman scholar and activist Morris writes, "It's not on me to have to prove my gentleness and my worth. I have no grace to extend and that's not my job." She stresses that she and her community will continue to be present for one another, "loving each other, fighting for freedom, and making our way to liberation" but that she needs to pass the mantle of explaining to white people how black people have dignity, and how black-led movements that fight for the dignity of black people have value. She instead exhorts white people to do that work: "Organize, mobilize, and strategize with and for *your* people. Work on uprooting white supremacy at your job, place of worship, and at the Thanksgiving."

I think part of taking up that noble-sounding work is also doing the less noble-sounding work of seeing oneself, as a white person, honestly. To see oneself honestly means, in part, to see oneself as raced and to see racial cruelty not only in the exceptional other, but here, in my own, communal, body. Oluo urges: "And as much as I'd like you to see me—as much as I'd like systemic racism to simply be a problem of different groups not seeing each other—I need you to see yourself, really see yourself, first. This is the top priority."[36] Because white people and POC live together, in a relationship, it is not enough to see the other without seeing oneself. Oluo says she understands why white people avoid seeing ourselves, but she does not understand what will make us give up that avoidance. People have color, she writes, have been trying to hold up a mirror to whiteness for a long time, only to be swatted away. "We've been begging you to see what you came from and the true legacy you have inherited. We've begged you to see your boot on our necks as long as it's been there."

1.2   "WE" WHITE PEOPLE: ON THE POSSIBILITY OF COLLECTIVE IDENTITY

I should clarify my terms. To adopt the name "white" is neither to give whiteness nor race in general metaphysical or fascist credence. Whiteness is not an ontological status because race is not ontological, metaphysical, or biological; it is social.[37] It is true that those who often claim whiteness as an ontological or metaphysical status are the white supremacists. Whiteness is not "special" in the way that those groups claim and there is no essential human nature tied to whiteness and no pre-ordained future for the white race. The history of the idea of race is fraught, of course: its nascence in the Enlightenment was inseparably tied to the economic development of the Atlantic Slave Trade, and so-called scientific ideas of race were covers to justify dehumanization.[38]

However, claims about white people's tendencies in the United States, for example their common reactions to black-led social movements, can be true in specific, meaningful ways, without validating race as a predictive human essence or pointing to whiteness as a scientific category. Race is "real" because people's perceptions of race have real social consequences. Those perceptions are mutable, not fixed, but they nevertheless appear on the scene as frustratingly intransigent.

That perceptions of race have so much sticking power is due, in large part, to their colonial inheritance, a hierarchy which announced the bourgeois white European as civilized and fully human, while colonial subjects, in Maria Lugones' words, "were judged as bestial and thus non-gendered, promiscuous, grotesquely sexual, and sinful."[39] For Lugones and other decolonial theorists, the colonial civilizing mission "was the euphemistic mask of brutal access to people's bodies through unimaginable exploitation, violent sexual violation, control of reproduction, and systematic terror."[40] These imagined, gendered, and racialized hierarchies reproduce themselves in modernity; their legacy traces itself on our bodies. Whiteness still becomes a marker of the "civilized", and in that way whiteness still works as a political project. Part of the project of granting ourselves full humanity is granting our own white family and friends empathy and the possibility for growth and change. Thus, the way in which whiteness most often essentializes race not in terms of self-reference but is other-oriented. It essentializes race at the same moment it denies it is doing so. In George Yancy's words, in exaggerating and distorting the black body, whiteness "fixes" black people "as beings who are not robustly trans-phenomenal".[41] Whiteness does not afford non-white people growth and change, as individuals or groups. Besides problematic practices of essentializing, there is also a sense in which race is, if not metaphysical, at least existential. The social consequences of race shape the bodies, souls, minds, and spirits of generations, in both humanizing and dehumanizing ways.

Not all consequences of race are negative. For instance, cultural solidarity among identity groups, like when I revel in my grandmother's cooking or feel relief in my mother tongue, can be wonderful, comforting, fulfilling. I will forever enjoy the quintessential WASP-y, midwestern casserole, 1950s style, consisting of heaps of Campbell's "cream of" soups, sodium content included. Connections to home, and people who grew up with the same cultural lexicon, is grounding and meaningful. However, of course, not all consequences of race are positive. Consider, in one instance among many, the way black people are can be discriminated against in a job search just for having a "black sounding" name.[42] Their perceived race can have real social consequences, over which they have little control. The social consequences to which white people can be subject are just as real, and often unseen. I am more likely to get an interview because I have a non-black sounding name, and I am unlikely to notice that particular form of advantage. The hiring teams do not have to be white supremacists to enact these kinds of biases; they can be well-meaning people of all backgrounds and races. One can do and say racist things without being a self-identified racist. At any rate, because these social consequences of race are real; race, and thus whiteness, is real in the social, but not biological or essential, way. Because whiteness is socially real, it can shape knowledge and ignorance.

Again, when someone calls me "white", I might reject it, because I take it as implying a collective guilt. However, sometimes whiteness can indeed be a neutral descriptor. Consider, for instance, the statement, "White people love singing along to the song 'Don't Stop Believing' by the band Journey." When I say this, I mean this as a fact. It's neither good nor bad. It's just true. It is "reasonable" in the way that a Humean would mean reason, as a statement about the world separate from praise or blame.[43]

Such a statement is not universal, but it does not need to be universal in order for it to be true. There could be a white person who hates the band Journey. Or the song might come through the speaker in a breakfast diner, instead of a piano bar, where it would be inappropriate to yell SOUTH DETROIT! at the top of one's lungs. Nevertheless, though exceptions clearly exist, they do not negate the general trend's veracity. Moreover, I'm unlikely to strongly object to owning a sense of "we" here, in terms of white people. If I were to count us here as a group, I am not accepting any sense of collective guilt or lumping the a-morals with the moral people. It is not morally blameworthy to love Journey (or so they say).

Other times, whiteness can be impugning. For example, when Oluo writes that she "had to learn how your police force was created to return black people to slavery and maintained to control brown and black populations to manufacture a false sense of white security", whiteness contains damning characteristics.[44] Here, whiteness is composed of fear, power-plays, and denial. This instance is when I am more likely to object to whiteness as a group descriptor. My first response to Oluo is probably defensiveness, to claim exception. If I am attached to a particular system she mentions, for example the police force, I am likely to say something along the lines of "a few bad apples do not spoil the basket".[45] Here is where I recall that it is usually only white supremacists who refer to "white solidarity" as a worthy societal goal, and there is no solidarity to be had with bad apples.

What else is at stake in using the "we" in the pejorative sense, gathering all white people together, the presumed "virtuous" with the "sinners"? When I speak about empathy in my undergraduate classes, my students, almost uniformly, reject the proposition that one should empathize with white supremacists. The response tends to be as follows: If I were asked to see myself in the so-called "bad apples", I would probably be more likely to empathize with them and that feels like a dangerous enterprise, because it is difficult to distinguish empathy from moral justification. Regardless, the bad apples do not deserve empathy. I have built an identity category based in negation; whatever I am, it is not like them. But also, perhaps I am afraid because I might see something in myself that is like them. We might be yoked. I might be responsible for the bad apple in ways I am unwilling to be, ways that would involve risk.

Thus, there is much at stake in saying "we" when referring to fellow white people: it threatens my self-image, affords undue justification, and implicates me in responsibility and risk. In order to take on such a name, then, we need a model for someone who assumed such risk. The southern writer Eudora Welty is, I think, a starting point for such a model. She is instructive. The way Welty writes gives one path to inhabiting the collective white "we". Welty's strength is that she avoids the disingenuous and puerile "white guilt" (and the so-called "white tears" and "white fragility"). She also shows how empathy can be disentangled from justification.

The night of Medgar Evers' 1963 murder, Welty, a fellow resident of Jackson, Mississippi, wrote a short fiction piece, entitled *Where is this Voice Coming From?*.[46] Written from the perspective of Evers' assassin, she explained that she was motivated to write it because, "I knew him. I knew him very well."[47] Welty did not mean she knew the actual assassin; she wrote her piece before Byron de la Beckwith was found and charged with Evers' murder. Rather, whomever he was, she knew his inner life, because it was the life of her friends and family, her white community. Byron de la Beckwith was not a pariah, but a man central to the white community. "What I was writing about really was that world of hate I felt I had grown up with and I felt I could speak as someone who knew it."[48]

Recalling the early Civil Rights movement, Welty spoke "unreality" of northern strangers calling her up at night, asking her to condemn southern apartheid. She found these entreaties so strange because, while she was against Jim Crow, she had been born out of it and knew it from the inside. Statements of "against", from the outside, seemed to her "so thin and artificial", because it disavowed the reality that she and the racists were not two communities.[49] They may disagree, but they were born from the same ground. Northern writing seemed to Welty merely "tracts" that knew, but did not admit to or own, the full horror of what makes up the white identity. As such, they were bad fiction. Welty's integration of the horror of racism into her own identity stands in contrast to Mrs. Williard, Ida Well's self-proclaimed ally who did not admit to the racist belief structure of the Northern Women's Temperance League. Welty is more mature, because she owns up to the dark places and brutality not just in her own being but in her own community. Her reaction is not denial, but, in knowing that it is possible for her to commit the horrors, asking what it would take for it to be prevented.

"Where is this Voice Coming From?" was so accurate that, when published, the New Yorker had to change the names and details so as not to affect Beckwith's trial. Welty's narrator drives to Evers' character's home because he heard him speaking on the radio (Evers was Mississippi's NAACP field secretary). Welty inhabits the executioner's voice: "I says to my wife, 'You can reach and turn it off. You don't have to set and look at a black nigger face no longer than you want to, or listen to what you don't want to hear. It's still a free country.'" The narrator emphasizes: One does not need to hear what one does not want. One does not need all reflections; some mirrors are disposable. No one can force him to be motivated to empathize. He is not compelled to give the movement the time of day, in Jones' words. The American ideal of freedom, for the narrator, is tied to this idea of turning people off, choosing some voices over others, and silencing some voices for good. That is what the American dream means for Welty's narrator and for white identity as well.

Again, how Welty writes is instructive for taking up the white "we". As the author, the narrator's reprehensible voice is, for a moment, her own voice. She may be ashamed and afraid that she can inhabit such a voice with such perspicuity, but she sees the whole enterprise to be a worthy one. Her anger at Ever's assassination inspires the writing, her work of understanding. The narrator's voice has no moral perspective, and there's no moral condemnation in the story itself. As Casey Sep writes, "Only hate has a voice in this story; morality is silent."[50] Where moral condemnation to be had, it falls upon the reader. Only the story's title addresses the reader directly, in a voice other than the narrator's: "Where is This Voice Coming From?" The reader is pressed to ask: is it mine? Our own community? The answer is affirmative, and the realization ends in horror. As a reader, I unearth anxiety when I find the degree to which I can, without effort, identify with the narrator. Like the Greek tragedies, a demand for change occurs not within the artistic work itself, but within its audience.[51] Welty places responsibility in the hands of her audience specifically by way of her ability to accurately size up the perpetrator, to understand him. Thus, empathy for the perpetrator is not inimical to moral condemnation but goes along with it. Of the story, Welty would later write, "A plot is a thousand times more unsettling than an argument, which may be answered."[52]

"Great fiction", Welty continued, "shows us not how to conduct our behavior but how to feel. Eventually, it may show us how to face our feelings and face our actions and to have new inklings about what they mean".[53] Welty's again uses the "we" here. Fiction shows *us* how to feel, shows us how to face *our* feelings. She does not separate, in Lebron's descriptions, the morally dim-witted from herself, the would-be liberal self-righteous. In inhabiting the racist narrator, Welty does not construct her own identity in terms of virtue, as if to say "my fiction tells *you* how to feel". In assuming the assassin's voice, she implies the opposite. She knows him, and in order not to be like him, I have to own up to the fact that he is me.

That ownership precludes me from virtue signaling. Anne Branigan writes that the "fulcrum of white identity isn't violence", as she had previously assumed. "It was virtue."[54] The reticence to adopt the universal "we" in whiteness comes, in part, from holding on to a sense of virtue. It is a virtue that maintains white supremacy, because the disavowal serves as a denial. Yet, in the vein of Welty, that sort of virtue of defining oneself against the true racists is shallow, thin, and artificial. It is the quietism of the self-satisfied defining oneself against the morally dim-witted. The reticence to say "we white people" is also, I think, immature, because it holds on to a certain false (but persistent) ignorance of the dark places inside ourselves and our communities. The value of owning up to darkness is not to perpetuate it but to understand it in order that the cycle is stopped.

Adopting the "we" in the name "white people" does not mean that all white people agree with one another, as it would be too literal-minded to claim that Welty as the author *agrees* with the reasoning of her racist narrator. She does not. Nor do I agree with, say, the white nationalist Richard Spencer when he talks about whiteness as a special essence. But the "we" does mean that we are family, we are birthed from the same ground, symbolically if not geographically, and "we" need to, as Morris exhorts, come get our people. And again, the "we" points to no specific or special essence. But saying "we" is acknowledging a sort of responsibility for one another. Collective guilt and collective responsibility are not the same and should not be conflated with one another.[55]

1.3   THE HATE THAT WE SEE MIGHT BE OUR OWN: DISTINGUISHING BLACK ANGER FROM WHITE HATE

If it is possible to posit a collective identity for white people in the United States without pointing to a special or scientific essence, it is therefore possible to make claims about trends in white people's reactions to black-led, democratic social movements for racial justice. The first "white" objection I address here is the quintessential comparison of BLM to the Civil Rights Movement on the basis of respectability politics. White people can tend to dismiss BLM based on its unrelation to our imagined Civil Rights Movement, the paragon of respectability. The objection usually goes something like this: "I *could* listen to BLM if it was, like the Civil Rights Movement, that is, more respectable."[56] Or, perhaps, "I could listen to BLM if it wasn't so filled with hate." The code words for more respectable include: less angry, less aggressive, less divisive, less incendiary, less courting of controversy, less criminal. This tactic of dismissal sets up a dichotomy between radical and respectable, where radical is taken to mean militant or violent. This objection relies on a mis-remembrance of the Civil Rights Movement, specifically forgetful of the content of the anger it expressed.

I want to make clear here, that when I talk about the Civil Rights movement in this chapter, I am talking primarily of the white misremembrance of it, the *doxic* imaginary of the Civil Rights. This white imaginary has very little to do with the actual movement, historically speaking, but a lot to do with how white people position themselves today and form our own identities in reference to our ideas about it. The movement itself was diverse, multifaceted. For one thing, its scholars and activists urge a fuller vision of Martin Luther King Jr. than the current white imaginary affords, a vision that includes his economic commitments and expansive critique of U.S. capitalism and militarism. Second, scholars and activists stress that the movement was much broader and more profound than can be encapsulated in one charismatic personality. King himself cautioned against reducing the movement to a single man. An excellent resource on this topic is *Putting the Movement Back into Civil Rights Teaching*, a K-12 teaching guide that Congressman John Lewis spearheaded, which introduces important and overlooked figures like Bayard Rustin and Ella Baker.[57] It emphasizes the contributions and leadership from women. *Putting the Movement Back* also recognizes that the Black Nationalism and Black Pride movements were part of, and not completely inimical to, Civil Rights.[58] Importantly, Civil Rights movement was not contained within the current white imaginary's reformist lens. Even the most so-called "respectable" of all black-led movements in the United States, was, too, revolutionary. BLM does not *only* draw from the Civil Rights legacies—it draws from anti-colonialism movements, global human rights, and abolition movements, to name a few—and there are points of sharp departure between the movements and times as well. But, in so far as it does draw from Civil Rights, it is in Civil Rights' visionary, revolutionary capacity.

The reason I interrogate the white imaginary of the Civil Rights here is because I am after what it is that the mis-remembrance *does*, in terms of forming and shaping white identity, in so far as that identity prevents us from affording due respect to BLM. What we belief about Civil Rights constructs the passive whiteness, the ideology, that shapes our own identities, even if these beliefs are inaccurate. One part of white, *doxic* memory of the Civil Rights' Movement, is that its sole inheritance is and should be that we should judge people by the content of their character. That claim functions as both a moral mandate and a past-tense accomplishment, simultaneously.[59] Somehow, since Martin Luther King Jr. made the declaration, it is both true that we *should* judge people this way and that we *already have*.[60] If we live in a colorblind society that has already achieved King's understood dream of merit-based judgment, we can more easily dismiss black-led movements for racial justice which point out, inconveniently, that many people of color's experiences do not confirm such a society, and we have not achieved that dream. One way such a dismissal works is to frame any message beyond merit-based judgment as radical, not respectable. It is as if all possible bounds of respectability began and ended on August 28, 1963. The position, then, becomes that BLM stands in contrast to the Civil Rights Movement; its activists are filled with hate and those whom BLM mourns died in rage.

Carol Anderson notes that the public and white discussion of the death of Michael Brown in 2014 and the police killing of other black people is framed in terms of black rage, manifesting itself in destructive and nonsensical ways. Of Ferguson, she notes, "commentators throughout the print and digital media served up variations of the same story: African Americans, angered by the police killing of an unarmed black teen, were taking out their frustration in unproductive and predictable ways—rampaging, burning, and looting."[61] Michael Brown was seen not as a teenager but a "thug" who just committed strong-armed robbery. The responses which frame black protest in terms of *only* black rage are one part of a larger project of respectability politics. Here, I mean by respectability politics what the Crunk Feminist Collective means:

> A nineteenth-century term and ideology, coined in the decades after slavery, which argues that if Black people acted chaste, pious, and frugal and comported themselves properly in public, they could prove their fitness for American citizenship. Today, respectability politics are often used to police Black people for nonnormative behavior.[62]

Respectability politics appear as common sense to many white people. Perhaps part of the reason why the particular quote about character has had such staying power as compared with the rest of King's legacy of racial and economic justice is that judging people by the "content of their character" gives permission, first, to judge. It gives license to white citizens to believe they can judge character fairly by various forms of social presentation. At any rate, current white *doxa* sees Martin Luther King as the paragon of respectability, even though the white public of the 1950s and 1960s did not see him this way. They saw him and his movement as radical and by radical they meant militant. Anderson writes that, "By 1966, 85 percent of whites were certain that 'the pace of civil rights progress was too fast'."[63] Some BLM activists have described their own movement as—in part, a demand for dignity on behalf of black people—one coming out of the frustration in the failure of aspirations to respectability. In *Beyond Respectability*, Brittney Cooper unravels dignity from respectability. Cooper writes that dignity is inherent, while demands for respectability assume that social propriety will prove one's dignity.[64] Respectability politics is useful for white supremacy, because the standards of respectability remain white, and they are all moving goal posts for people of color.

And yet, BLM is indeed radical, but not in the way the white *doxa* frames it. Lebron writes that BLM is radical precisely because it disrupts accepted modes of respectability. "Radicalism", under this definition, is "the imagination and will to think and act outside the bounds of the morally acceptable".[65] Radicalism does not necessarily entail militant stridency but instead a vision for comprehensively other social formations, drastically better worlds. As I discuss in Chap. 4, "Radical" means visionary, in the sense of being able to imagine the unprecedented. Under Lebron's account, BLM re-directs the missives of shame that are directed, under the banner of respectability politics, at black-led social movements and black people. BLM takes this shame and turns around, like a boomerang, back upon the democratic public. The movement destabilizes norms of acceptability.

BLM activists have taken Carol Anderson's warning about black respectability to heart. Anderson cautions that "attempts to present whites with a persona that is beyond judgment and beyond reproach in order to successfully navigate the various pitfalls and disadvantages blacks otherwise face in a society littered with white privilege" are a mirage.[66]

> Black respectability of "appropriate" behavior doesn't seem to matter. If anything, black achievement black aspirations, and black success are construed as direct threats. Obama's presidency made that clear. Aspirations and the achievement of these aspirations provide no protection. Not even to the God fearing.[67]

Learning the lesson well, BLM, has, in large part, divested themselves of attempts to conform to impossible standards, partly out of disillusionment and partly out of pragmatism. But just because BLM disregards respectability politics' demands for politeness and restraint, it does not mean that the movement is hateful. If we white people see hate in black-led social movements, the hate that we see is, in large part, our own.

We tend to translate anger of all kinds in black-led social movements, sometimes righteous anger translating as rage, sometimes anger in public mourning as hate. Although anger can sometimes manifest as hate, as they are not mutually exclusive feelings. Thus, if white people translate *all* or *most* of the anger they see in black-led social movements as hate, it is worth asking ourselves why we do that. In other words, if we interpret all messages outside of the "judging by content of character", if the mistranslation is so persistent, we should ask: what accounts for the roots of that hermeneutic gap. For instance, the relevant point here is not that "Black Lives Matter" does not, in fact, mean "white lives do not matter." That point has been made, over and over again.[68] Instead, the relevant question to ask here is why is a white public so quick to assume an "instead" clause and so persistently deny a "too", after "black lives matter"? In other words, the question here is not why statements like "All Lives Matter" or "Blue Lives Matter" miss the point, but rather, *why* is there an obstinate clinging to "All Lives Matter" even after the point has been made? Why does that form of white ignorance persist, fight back, even after reasonable persuasion, explanation, and civil discourse? I think the reason is because we mostly will/do not face the hate in our own communities, and so the hate we attribute to black-led social movements becomes projection. So, when we hear voices of hate, we might, like Welty, ask "Where is this voice coming from?"

Unraveling white hate from black anger accords with Anderson's thesis that black advancement in the United States after slavery has been hampered by white rage, not black anger. Anderson writes that white rage is, for a white public, harder to see, because it does not always manifest explicitly.

> White rage is not about visible violence, but rather it works its way through the courts, the legislatures, and a range of government bureaucracies. It wreaks havoc subtly, almost imperceptibly. Too imperceptibly, certainly, for a nation consistently drawn to the spectacular—to what it can *see*. It's not the Klan. White rage doesn't have to wear sheets, burn crosses, or take to the streets. Working the halls of power, it can achieve its ends far more effectively, far more destructively.[69]

Anderson submits that the shape of white rage has come in the forms of backlash to Reconstruction reforms, Brown vs. Board of Education, the Civil Rights Movement, and Obama's presidency. I think white rage is also manifest in backlash to BLM. Hateful rage does not need to appear in the form of open expression of emotion. Indeed, the subtler white rage is, the more it can be effective. BLM, on the other hand, is, as I discuss in Chap. 3, expressive. It breaks the bounds of respectability politics by opening the space for the whole range of human emotion, including, but not limited to, anger.

Audre Lorde best distinguishes hate from anger. In *The Uses of Anger*, Lorde begins by recounting an experience of speaking at a feminism conference, in which a white woman asked her to "tell me how you feel but don't say it too harshly or I cannot hear you".[70] Lorde wonders if it is her manner that keeps her interlocutor from hearing or if that excuse is a cover up for the fear this lady might feel that the content of Lorde's message might require a change or sacrifice. She advises that white women change our approach: that we listen to the content of what is being said with as much intensity as we defend ourselves from the form in which it arrives.

First, Lorde contends that hatred and anger have different goals: the end of hatred is destruction, while the end of anger is change. Anger, for Lorde, is both a display and a distortion of grief. If directed, anger can be a creative force; it is generative and instructive. Like other negative emotions, anger carries important information. It also carries energy. As a force, it can be usefully harnessed. It gives momentum to interactions and movements. Lorde does not go so far as to claim that anger is equivalent to moral authority. Nevertheless, she cautions that it is distinct from solely an expression of suffering, "What you hear in my voice", she insists, "is fury, not suffering". In instances where black anger is not automatically dismissed as hate, white people tend to interpret it in a way to lessen its charge, by understanding it as oppression or suffering. This interpretation robs anger's energy, its force. The misinterpretation reminds me of the way Hurston describes the prevailing reception of her book: as only an expression of suffering and not a full literary work on the whole range of human emotion, including joy. The interpretation of anger as suffering gives a tone of claustrophobia to the interaction—it constrains the range of possible communication and makes it easier to escape the space and keep talking. This false constraint is unfortunate, because anger is, for Lorde, first and foremost, a form of communication. "If I speak to you in anger, at least I have spoken to you: I have not put a gun to your head and shot you down in the street; I have not looked at your bleeding sister's body and asked, 'What did she do to deserve it?'" Seen as communication, anger can take the form of a plea, a call, a proclamation or affirmation. When I am trying to talk to you, I am not trying to make you suffer. I am not inflicting vengeance upon you. Anger is rarely hate, a manifested dismissal of someone's human dignity. Unlike anger, hate is not communication.

Crucially, "Anger is an appropriate reaction to racist attitudes, as is fury when the actions arising from those attitudes do not change." Conversely, to respond to racism, for Lorde, means responding to her own anger, the "anger of exclusion, of unquestioned privilege, of racial distortions, of silence, ill-use, stereotyping, defensiveness, misnaming, betrayal, and co-optation". Lorde is making a space here for anger and its expressions.

Brittney Cooper's autobiography *Eloquent Rage* works within Lorde's legacy.[71] Cooper admits that it is a dangerous thing to "own your anger" if you are a black woman, and that for years, even though she was indeed angry, she did not want to admit to being so, in order that she would not be stereotyped as an "angry black woman". But she realized that her scholarship and activism was indeed shaped by rage, a useful and pointed kind. She describes realizing this young woman: "Even though I was only in my mid-twenties at the time, I had already experienced many years of white people doing that thing they do to articulate Black women—always asking us 'Why are you so angry?' I hated the accusation from others, usually white people, because it was unfair, a way to discredit the legitimacy of the things Black women say by calling them emotional and irrational." In self-reflection, Cooper affords herself rationality in her anger. While her white interlocutors insisted on the dichotomy between rationality and emotion, Cooper describes a process of unraveling that dichotomy, in order to find and claim her own power.

I want to contrast Lorde's and Cooper's affirmation of anger-as-communication and fully appropriate response to racism with Martha Nussbaum's rejection of anger, in her theory of Martin Luther King and the Civil Rights movement. Unlike Lorde, Nussbaum does not think anger is publicly useful. Under Nussbaum's evolving account of emotions, there are some emotions that should be publicly cultivated in law and social movements and some emotions which should be left to the side. Anger is in the latter category. I take up Nussbaum here because her philosophical formations, like other liberals, are mirrors of the common white liberal *doxa* about black anger contained within a mis-remembering of Civil Rights. As such, she reads respectability politics into King and conflates anger with hate. Contra Lorde, Nussbaum does not see a communicative and transformative power in anger and thus her reading of King constrains its radicality. Nussbaum's reading of King is important, because if Nussbaum is right about King's lack of anger, white liberals could more accurately claim distinguishable grounds of disunion between the Civil Rights Movement and BLM and thus BLM's justified dismissal.

Nussbaum's broad thesis here is that "Anger is not an essential part of combatting injustice."[72] She supports this claim based, in part, on an appeal to Martin Luther King. "Following the writings of … Martin Luther King, Jr., that anger is not only not necessary for the pursuit of justice, but also a large impediment to the generosity and empathy that help to construct a future of justice."[73] In the parlance of ancient drama, Nussbaum argues that if the furies are to have a place in public life, they must undergo a fundamental transformation before they make their appearance. Anger, defined as an animalistic and wild desire for retribution, should be replaced by forward-looking hope and compassion, and as these emotions are receptive to the voice of persuasion. In terms of anger, there is not a need for those dark places in our lives to make an appearance in the public square.

Nussbaum defines anger as: "A retaliatory and hopeful outward movement that seeks the pain of the offender *because of and as a way of assuaging or compensating for* one's own pain."[74] Here, there is an ambiguity in Nussbaum's writing. It is unclear if she defines all anger as vengeful, or if she specifies vengeful anger as one type of anger, which has no place in public life, whereas presumably other types of anger, such as the righteous kind, would have a place. Because Nussbaum speaks about anger's transformation as foundational, it seems more the case that all forms of anger need to be transformed into hopeful compassion, if they are to be just.

Nussbaum gives a reading of King's 1963 "I Have a Dream" speech to support her thesis that anger must be transformed in public life. Anger in public movements like Civil Rights is at most a concession, an allowance for people to blow off steam, but not a force that can spark meaning.[75] It must be quickly channeled into more positive emotions. She writes that, in so far as King allowed for some anger in public protests, it was as a way of channeling repressed emotions that might otherwise lead to violence.[76] "Nonetheless", for Nussbaum, "even when there is real anger, it must soon lead to a focus on the future, with hope and with faith in the possibility of justice."[77] Public life—law and social movements—must primarily be future oriented. There is little space for retribution for past wrongs here. Nussbaum also interprets King's pursuit of self-purity, by way of a study of Gandhi, to mean rejection of anger. Beyond nonviolence, Nussbaum claims that King was espousing non-anger as well.

If, as Lorde writes, part of her anger is always "libation for her fallen sisters", and if we consider, as Rankine does, that BLM is a movement of mourning, one cannot categorize either Lorde's or BLM's anger as *merely* future oriented. Rather, these social movements are in some ways about changing the future through recognizing the past, transforming trauma. Nussbaum's demand that social movements be only future oriented seems to miss the power in the black-led social movements Lorde and Rankine describe. Further, future-oriented hope is inextricable tied up with anger. I tend to be most angry when I am disappointed, specifically disappointed that the future I hoped for, even expected, is presently being denied. The categorical distinction Nussbaum makes between past, present, and future does not correspond, phenomenologically, to the shape of all anger.

Nussbaum notes that King begins his speech in a tone of anger, speaking of the past, "One hundred years after the Emancipation Proclamation, 'the life of the Negro is still sadly crippled by the manacles of segregation and the chains of discrimination.'" Then Nussbaum reads King's next move—comparing white people to bankers who have defaulted on a financial obligation—as a move away from demonizing white people to cooperatively engaging them. King: "America has given the Negro people a bad check, a check which has come back marked 'insufficient funds.'" Nussbaum reads King here as moving away from retribution, because one cannot wish retribution on one's debtor if one wishes them to pay you back. Furthermore, paying back a debt is supposed to spark unity between blacks and whites, a kind of unity where everyone's boat is lifted in freedom's rising tide. "So the 'payback' is reconceived as the paying of a debt, a process that unites black and white in a quest for freedom and justice. Everyone benefits: as many white people already recognize, 'their freedom is inextricably bound to our freedom.'"[78] In the movement toward universal brotherhood, Nussbaum stresses, "The essential question is not how whites can be humiliated."[79]

I must pause here for a moment and ask why it is that Nussbaum assumes that humiliating whites was *ever* the question, on the minds of King and his audience? It is an odd assumption, but the strangeness of it could be missed because the move is, at the same time, so familiar. Why is it that white people so often read all anger expressed in black-led social movements as vengeful? We see the same move when we respond to "Black Lives Matter" with assertions that "All Lives Matter." Again, why does saying "Black Lives Matter" mean, to white people, that all lives do not matter? The assumption that the content of anger expressed in democratic social movements is mostly vengeful is, in most cases, an interpretive error. However, it is an error that gives information about the interpreter.

That a white public sees vengeance in righteous anger is because, on some level, white people know that our own legacy of slavery is one of humiliation and undermining the dignity of black people; we know that one aim of our own anti-black racism is to humiliate, and we assume that the anger we read at the beginning of King's speech, or in the demand that black lives matter, is a threat that the chickens are soon coming home to roost. In misunderstanding anger as hate vis-à-vis projection, we take the anger expressed in black-led social movements to mean the same thing as our own history of hate.

Of course, Nussbaum does distinguish hate from anger. She follows Aristotle (and Lorde) in believing that destruction—ceasing to exist—is the only thing that will satisfy hate.[80] Anger's vengeful character does not necessarily imply a wish to see the other cease to exist; it is a wish to see the other suffer as they have suffered. Nussbaum also distinguishes anger from contempt, an attitude that views another as base.[81] Yet, she still in some measure conflates [white people's historical] hate with [black-led social movements'] anger. Again, why assume that anger primarily consists in a desire for retribution? Anger could have other content: frustration of not being heard, at injustice's staying power, a hope for a different future, or in Lorde's case, love for one's fallen sisters, a sense of solidarity. Nussbaum describes the transition from which King brought his audience as one *from* retribution *to* brotherhood. In her reading, such is King's ark. She associates retribution with the bitterness and hatred of which King spoke, when he urged, "Let us not seek to satisfy our thirst for freedom by drinking from the cup of bitterness and hatred ... Again and again, we must rise to the majestic heights of meeting physical force with soul force."[82] Nussbaum sees King as the kind of leader that is taking his audience from sin to salvation. King is the individual hero who rescues his ignorant audience, bent on revenge. The story would change a bit if the audience was not, in the first place, gathered for retribution.

For Lorde, in contrast, anger can be a "soul force". Interpreted as "libation for my fallen sisters", anger is not, strictly speaking, revenge. It is something more like mourning, more like honoring the dead than wishing others' death, more like desire for change than destruction. Read as communication—"at least I am still talking to you"—anger is not, again, mere vindictiveness. It is a form of engagement, not a dismissal. Importantly, Lorde's anger is completely *reasonable*. Anger is not only receptive to persuasion, it is itself a form of persuasion. Yet, anger is not persuasion detached from an emotional experience of one's body and of the world. Under Lorde's account, anger has and needs a place in public life, because it carries essential information. This information is, at various times, about mourning, about indignation, and about both the shape of injustice and how to change it. For Lorde, anger is both a motivator for change and, contra Nussbaum, a guide for change's direction.

Nussbaum returns to King, again, reinforcing the alternative picture of universal brotherhood as revenge. She writes, "One might imagine a future of pay-back, in which African-Americans would attain power and inflict retributive pain and humbling on white Americans. Society abounded with such ideas, despite the fact payback of that type would have made things no better and a lot worse. King's altogether superior stance was that the Transition is only a heartbeat away, since only cooperation will really solve the nation's problems."[83] Nussbaum starts here by positing that "One might imagine". Who is the owner of the imagination here? It is white people. It is those who might listen to the whole of King's speech, expecting to hear echoes of retribution, and be relieved by its absence. It sounds like King's FBI minders. However, I would contend, the imagination here is not King's nor his African-American audience. Putting the matter in terms of a debt does not request a pound of flesh, but neither is it a picture in which, as Nussbaum contends, "everyone benefits", black and white the same. If I am forced to give back money I owe, I do not, strictly speaking, benefit. In fact, I have to sacrifice some measure of unadulterated self-interest. If my creditor does not have the power to demand the money back, all the better for me; I get to keep more money. It is in my interest to invalidate my creditor's claims. Moreover, if I am on the other end of the transaction and someone fails to pay me back, I figure that is as good of reason as any to be mad. I am mad because this person is not fair or just. King's vision of universal brotherhood demands sacrifice on the part of white people, to give up benefits and unearned privilege. But again, this demand is distinguishable from retribution.

Sacrifice is not retribution, because I sacrifice for the people I care about and with whom I am in a relationship. Sacrifice involves my willing consent and agency, and if I am suffering, it is not at the hands of someone else. Nussbaum's reading of King downplays the sacrifice and gives a liberal, beatific "mountaintop moment" that, contra King, does not demand enough from white people. Because it is only forward-looking, it does not demand a self-reflection that is a reckoning with our own past.

Nussbaum also assumes that empathy is only possible in the absence of anger. Lorde's anger-as-communication is an opportunity for empathy to exist within anger. Nussbaum contends that "non-anger is … linked to practices that support empathetic participation in the lives of others. This was also a prominent feature of King's movement, in which blacks and whites associated together in defiance of law, and in which white supporters were constantly urged to imagine the indignities and hardships of a black person's life."[84] Nussbaum's account assumes that if black people are angry, white people cannot or will not empathize. That assumption is false, as I discuss in the proceeding chapters. Granted, it is much harder to empathize with a person who is currently expressing anger toward me. But it is not impossible. It is precisely the assumption that I cannot empathize with anger that gets me off the hook for spending my time *trying* to empathize. When I assume that empathy is impossible with anger, I can allow myself to think that this particular interaction, this relationship, is "not worth my time".

However, Nussbaum's axiomatic assumption that anger precludes empathy forecloses the possibility of asking a vital question: *can black anger ever mean love for any future in which whites can form coalition*?[85] I do not know the answer to that question; it motivates this book. I certainly hope white people can form a political project that recognizes black anger—if we could, we can start new histories, alchemize colonial legacies that prevent us from affording non-whites a full range of feelings, full humanity. We could stop trying to cauterize the political power of embodied emotions. For now, I can only say that *if* white coalition with black anger is possible, it can only be so if white people take a hard look at our reactions which prevent solidarity, before the fact. I also need to ask: if coalition is imaginable, under what conditions might it be possible?

In the summer of 2016, after Philando Castile and Alton Sterling were killed, a Houston BLM chapter held a vigil around the Martin Luther King statue in MacGregor Park. Community activist Ashton P. Woods brought a loud speaker and passed around a microphone to whomever wanted to talk. The group gathered, opening an outlet for people to express how they felt at that moment, what they were going through. I remember a range of expression, from a guided meditation encouraging compassion through breath to plans for an economic support of local black-led businesses, as well as strong anger, fear, sadness, and frustration. There was a news anchor present from a local ABC affiliate, Chauncy Glover, whom I like a lot—a year later, he would end up helping a woman through labor, live on TV, during the floods from Hurricane Harvey. I noticed Glover was assigned to cover a number of BLM protests and vigils over the years. I wondered what part of this protest would make it on the evening news, if the producers thought explicitly about editing out the expressions of strong anger, in anticipation of a white public's reaction. I imagine my white colleagues and family not present at the protest but catching snippets in passing, making dinner, or driving. If encountered through that medium, passively taking in information on the way to flipping channels or putting a casserole in the oven, would they be responsive to strong expressions of black anger on behalf of slain innocents? No. I know they would not. But if, by some shift I do not know how to inspire, my family came to the vigil, not just once but over time, if they found that turning worth their time, they might start to see who it is who is expressing anger. They might start to love the kind of future that BLM tries to create.

But here I am, present at some—not all—of these protests. I wonder, then, if it is just self-righteousness to divert my gaze to family and friends, when I am the one witnessing these moments. I should ask myself: do I love this future? Can I respect black anger (and joy, and all the other public emotions) enough to be in solidarity with its political project? That is a harder question. I find myself wanting so quickly to say yes, unequivocally, like children raising their hand as tall as they can when the teacher poses a question to the class. But that quickness, that surety of that jump to the affirmative, feels like I have something to prove. I suspect it is that leap to claim white virtue, to show I am one of the "good ones". So, I become unsure if I can be as honest about my response as question's candor demands. My "good girl" ambitions get in the way. Do I even understand the question?

I start again. If I have love, it is pale. It does not contain the depth with which activists love their brothers and sisters, or certainly, with which parents love their children. Can I hold space for the expression of anger, even rage, at a future cut short, the disappointments from a promised future not yet arrived, if my own white future is coming along just fine? As I struggle through this question, I am realizing that any answer I try to give to this question is trite and striving. Any kind of authentic reply may not be for me to give. When I think about how I show love to my own family, whether or not I claim I love someone matters a lot less than when someone feels loved. And my sister or son do not always need to tell me that they feel loved, either, they just need to be doing well. My best self [not always the person who shows up day-to-day] wants them to be secure in the knowledge that I am here for them, to walk with them and make space for whoever they are, as they are, for their dark emotions as well as the light. I would like that best self to show up when I try to respond to black-led political speech and action. Whether BLM activists feel loved or not, whether they are doing well, is not for me, or for the white public at large, to say. The proof is when black people feel their own lives matter.

So, back to unraveling white defenses: the white mis-remembrance of Civil Rights that shuts out anger for the purpose of minimizing BLM's moral impact is a political and ideological project, not a fact. Both BLM and the Civil Rights Movement are and were radical; neither are they polite. They express a righteous anger. In such anger, both movements convey what Cooper calls "eloquent rage"—a communication calling for a reckoning. That communication is not hate. White people mistake it for hate and retribution because we are so mired in our own history of humiliating black populations. When we refuse to listen to black-led social movements, and black people, because they are too "angry", we project our own hate onto these dignified and rational calls for a new and better future.

I want to conclude with three quotes from King's "I have a Dream Speech" that are not the beatific moments white liberals point to as inciting colorblindness but are nonetheless important expressions of dignified anger. There is no need for a social movement to "transition", in the words of Nussbaum, out of this anger, unless more just social arrangements transition as well. King's words—"rude awakening", the threat of "neither rest nor tranquility", the promise of a "whirlwind of revolt" meant to shake not an accidental racist outlier but "the foundation of America"—highlight his radicality and the reality that even the paragon of white respectability never conformed to those standards in the first place. There is no sense in which King's anger is "blowing off steam", considered as a phase. Moreover, it is wrong of white people to expect BLM to divest itself of anger before we can listen.

> *This sweltering summer of the Negro's legitimate discontent will not pass until there is an invigorating autumn of freedom and equality—1963 is not an end but a beginning. Those who hope that the Negro needed to blow off steam and will now be content will have a rude awakening if the nation returns to business as usual.*

> *There will be neither rest nor tranquility in America until the Negro is granted his citizenship rights. The whirlwind of revolt will continue to shake the foundation of America until the bright days of justice emerge.*

> *There are those who are asking the devotees of civil rights, "When will you be satisfied?" We can never be satisfied as long as the Negro is the victim of the unspeakable horrors of police brutality.*

NOTES

1. William Shakespeare, *King Lear*, Act. 1, Scene 1.
2. Ida B. Wells-Barnett, "A Red Record" in *On Lynching* (Mineola: Dover, 2014), 29–116.
3. Janine Jones, "The Impairment of Empathy in Goodwill Whites for African Americans", in George Yancy (ed.) *What White Looks Like: African American Philosophers on the Whiteness Question* (New York: Routledge, 2004), 66.

4. Linda Martín Alcoff gives a full history of the concept of whiteness, both internationally and in the United States, in *The Future of Whiteness* (Cambridge: Polity, 2015).

5. This is Thomas Chatterton Williams' position, that if one affirms whiteness, one allows for whites to possess a collective essence or specialness, harkening back to German Fascism and the durability of white supremacy. See Williams' "How Ta-Nahesi Coates Gives Whiteness Power", *The New York Times*. October 6, 2017. https://www.nytimes.com/2017/10/06/opinion/ta-nehisi-coates-whiteness-power.html

6. For a discussion of Aristotelean methods, see G.E.L. Owens, "Tιθέναι Ta Φαινόμena", In Moravcsik J.M.E. (eds) *Aristotle. Modern Studies in Philosophy* (London: Palgrave Macmillan, 1967).

7. Ijeoma Oluo, "White People: I want you to Understand Yourself Better", *Medium*, February 7, 2017, https://medium.com/the-establishment/white-people-i-dont-want-you-to-understand-me-better-i-want-you-to-understand-yourselves-a6fbedd42ddf

8. Ibid.

9. See George Yancy's collected volume, "*White Self-Criticality Beyond Anti-Racism*: How does it Feel to be a White Problem?" (New York: Lexington, 2014).

10. Claudia Rankine, *Citizen: An American Lyric* (Minneapolis: Graywolf Press, 2014) 135.

11. Rankine, The Condition of Black Life is One of Mourning. The New York Times, June 22, 2015. https://www.nytimes.com/2015/06/22/magazine/the-condition-of-black-life-is-one-of-mourning.html

12. Rankine, "The Condition of Black Lives is One of Mourning", *The New York Times*, June 22, 2015. https://www.nytimes.com/2015/06/22/magazine/the-condition-of-black-life-is-one-of-mourning.html

13. For thorough discussion, see Linda Martín Alcoff's essay "Epistemologies of Ignorance: Three Types", in *Race and Epistemologies of Ignorance*, Shannon Sullivan and Nancy Tuana, eds. (New York: SUNY Press, 2007) See also Alison Bailey's "Strategic Ignorance" in the same volume.

14. Jones, "Impairment of Empathy", 67.

15. Sonam Sheth, "White Supremacist in Charlottesville: I am not the Angry Racist you see in that Photo", *Business Insider*, August 14, 2017. https://www.businessinsider.com/peter-cvjetanovic-white-supremacist-charlottesville-photo-not-angry-racist-2017-8

16. Jones, "Impairment of Empathy", 68.

17. For more on the distinction between ideal and non-ideal political theory and ideal theory's impediment to racial justice, see Naomi Zack, "Ideal, Non-Ideal, and Empirical Theories of Justice: The Need for Applicative Justice in Addressing Injustice", in The Oxford Handbook of Philosophy and Race (Oxford: Oxford UP, 2017).

18. Jones, "Impairment of Empathy", 69.
19. Ibid.
20. Ibid., 76.
21. bell hooks speaks extensively to this phenomena, in *Ain't I a Woman: Black Women and Feminism* (New York, Routledge, 2014); as does George Yancy in the introduction to *White Self-Criticality*. Yancy writes, "those white people who want to continue the dominant-subordinate relationship so endemic to racist exploitation by insisting that we 'serve' them—that we do the work of challenging and changing their consciousness—are acting in bad faith" (6).
22. Christopher Lebron, *The Making of Black Lives Matter: A Brief History of an Idea* (Oxford: Oxford UP, 2017).
23. Ibid., 139.
24. Ibid., 153–154.
25. I mean by epistemic justice what Miranda Fricker means in *Epistemic Justice: Power and the Ethics of Knowing* (Oxford, Oxford UP, 2007).
26. Lebron, *The Making of Black Lives Matter*, 155.
27. I witnessed much of activists' expression vis-a-vis The Shout Poetry Collective, 2015, and also a panel on Intersectional Activism, International Peace Day, September 21, 2015. Rice University.
28. Ayan Abdulle, "An Exploratory Paper on Understanding Whiteness", *New Framings on Anti-Racism and Resistance*. Vol. 1. Ayan Abdulle and Anne Nelun Obeyesekere, eds. (Rotterdam: Sense, 2017) 23.
29. Claudia Rankine, "Bleached Racists and Lynching Trees: The Show that's Targeting White Supremacy", *The Guardian*. August 10, 2018. https://www.theguardian.com/artanddesign/2018/aug/10/bleached-racists-lynching-trees-the-show-thats-targeting-white-supremacy-on-whiteness-claudia-rankine
30. Sara Ahmed, "A Phenomenology of Whiteness", *Feminist Theory*, 2007, 8:149.
31. See Eduardo Bonilla-Silva, *Racism without Racists Color-Blind Racism and the Persistence of Racial Inequality in America* (NY: Rowman & Littlefield 2017).
32. Rankine, "Bleached Racists and Lynching Trees: The Show that's Targeting White Supremacy", *The Guardian*. August 10, 2018. https://www.the-guardian.com/artanddesign/2018/aug/10/bleached-racists-lynching-trees-the-show-thats-targeting-white-supremacy-on-whiteness-claudia-rankine
33. Thomas Chatterton William's Twitter feed, Feb. 13, 2019. https://twitter.com/thomaschattwill/status/1095715271497707526
34. Lebron, *The Making of Black Lives Matter*, 163.
35. Susana M. Morris, "After the love has gone: radical community after the election", in *The Crunk Feminist Collection*. Britney C. Cooper, Susana

M. Morris, and Robin M. Boylorn, eds. (New York: The Feminist Press, 2017).

36. Oluo, "White People".
37. For a thorough debate on the relative "realness" of race, see Joshua Glasgow, *A Theory of Race* (New York: Routledge, 2009).
38. For a complete account of the history of the pseudo-science of race, see Naomi Zack, *The Philosophy of Science and Race* (New York: Routledge, 2002).
39. Maria Lugones, "Toward a Decolonial Feminism", *Hypatia*, Vol 24: 4. 2010. 743.
40. Ibid.
41. Yancy, *White Self-Criticality*, 39.
42. Marianne Bertrand, Sendhil Mullainathan, "Are Emily and Greg More Employable than Lakisha and Jamal? A Field Experiment on Labor Market Discrimination", *The National Bureau of Economic Research*, Working Paper No. 9873, July 2003, http://www.nber.org/papers/w9873
43. David Hume's explanation of reason as distinguished from praise or blame comes in part IV of *A Treatise on Human Nature*, "Of Skepticism with Regard to Reason."
44. Oluo, "White People".
45. For instance, Attorney General Jeff Sessions referred to abusive police as "bad apples". See Adam Serwer, "Jeff Session's Blind Eye", *The Atlantic*, April 5, 2017.
46. Eudora Welty, "Where is this Voice Coming From?", *The New Yorker*, July 6, 1963.
47. Eudora Welty, interview with William F. Buckley for *Firing Line*, "The Southern Imagination", The Hoover Institution, Stanford University. Dec. 12, 1972 https://www.youtube.com/watch?v=6RoWFb2pgjE
48. Ibid.
49. Ibid.
50. Casey N. Sep, "A Murder in Deep Summer", *The New Yorker*, July 18, 2013.
51. Oliver Taplin, *Greek Tragedy in Action* (London and New York: Routledge, 2000) 117–125.
52. Eudora Welty, "Must the Novelist Crusade?", *the Atlantic*, 1965.
53. Ibid.
54. Anne Branigan, "Why 2017 Was the Year of Rose Armitage", *The Root*, December 24, 2017. https://www.theroot.com/why-2017-was-the-year-of-rose-armitage-1821137750, in *Good White People*, Shannon Sullivan also extensively critiques the notion of white virtue.
55. A thorough distinction between guilt and responsibility is outside the scope of this paper. Iris Marion Young's theorizes it well in *Responsibility for Justice* (Oxford: Oxford UP, 2011).

56. Mark Lilla makes a version of this claim in *The Once and Future Liberal: After Identity Politics* (New York: Harper, 2017). I address Lilla's objection to identity politics and Black Lives Matter's tactics at length in Chap. 5.

57. *Putting the Movement Back in Civil Rights: A Resource Guide for Classrooms and Communities.* Deborah Menkart, Alana D. Murray, and Jenice L View, eds. (New York: Teaching for Change, 2004). see also https://www.civilrightsteaching.org/

58. See also Peniel E. Joseph, *Waiting 'Til the Midnight Hour: A Narrative History of Black Power in America* (New York: Holt) 2007. Also, Cornel West's introduction to Martin Luther King, Jr. *The Radical King* (New York: Beacon, 2016).

59. Both Alfred Frankowski and Charles Mills have made versions of claim about "post-racialism". See Frankowski, *The Post-Racial Limits of Memorialization: Towards a Political Sense of Mourning* (Lanham: Lexington Books, 2015) and Mills, *Black Rights/White Wrongs: The Critique of Racial Liberalism* (Oxford: Oxford UP, 2017).

60. Carol Anderson describes the Reagan-era interpretation of Lyndon Johnson's great society in this paradox. Anderson, *White Rage: The Unspoken Truth of our Racial Divide* (London and New York: Bloomsbury, 2016) 101.

61. Ibid., 2.

62. Index of terms, *Crunk Feminist Collection*, Brittney C. Cooper, Susana M. Morris, and Robin M. Boylorn, eds. (NY: The Feminist Press, 2017) 328.

63. Anderson, *White Rage*, 22.

64. Brittney Cooper, *Beyond Respectability: The Intellectual Thought of a Race Woman* (Champaign: University of Illinois Press, 2017).

65. Lebron, *Black Lives Matter*, xx.

66. Ibid., 135.

67. Anderson, *White Rage*, 159.

68. See, for instance, Daniel Victor, "Why 'All Lives Matter' is such a Perilous Phrase", *The New York Times*, July 15, 2016. https://www.nytimes.com/2016/07/16/us/all-lives-matter-black-lives-matter.html; Ian Olosov, How Did "All Lives Matter" Come to Oppose "Black Lives Matter"? A Philosopher of Language Weighs In, *Slate*, July 18, 2016. http://www.slate.com/blogs/lexicon_valley/2016/07/18/all_lives_matter_versus_black_lives_matter_how_does_the_philosophy_of_language.html; Elle Hunt, "Alicia Garza on the Beauty and Burden of Black Lives Matter", *The Guardian*, Sept. 2, 2016. https://www.theguardian.com/us-news/2016/sep/02/alicia-garza-on-the-beauty-and-the-burden-of-black-lives-matter

69. Anderson, *White Rage*, 3.

70. Audre Lorde, "The Uses of Anger", *Women's Studies Quarterly*, Vol. 25, No. ½. Spring/Summer 1997. http://blogs.ubc.ca/hopeprinceengl470a/files/2016/10/audre-lorde.pdf

71. Brittney Cooper, *Eloquent Rage*: A Black Feminist Discovers her Superpower (New York: St. Martin's, 2018).

72. Marth Nussbaum, *Anger and Forgiveness: Resentment, Generosity, and Justice* (Oxford: Oxford UP, 2016).

73. Ibid., 8.

74. Ibid., 31.

75. Ibid., 218.

76. Ibid., 52.

77. Ibid., 52.

78. Ibid., 31.

79. Ibid., 31.

80. Aristotle, *Nichomachean Ethics*, 1382a15.

81. Nussbaum, *Anger and Forgiveness*, 50.

82. Martin Luther King, Jr. "I Have a Dream…", 1963 March on Washington. https://www.archives.gov/files/press/exhibits/dream-speech.pdf

83. Nussbaum, *Anger and Forgiveness*, 39.

84. Ibid., 223.

85. I thank Alfred Frankowski for framing the question this way. I use his exact phrasing because of the power of the question.

CHAPTER 2

Empathy and Racial Justice: Redefining Impartiality in Response to Social Movements

2.1   White Empathy and Black Lives Matter

When I (a white woman from a middle-class background) began to attend Black Lives Matter protests in and around the Houston area in 2014, white friends and colleagues would ask about the movement. Why, for instance, did people protest in the Galleria, the most populous mall area in Houston when it was really the police that needed reform, and not the commercial sector? Why did the protestors feel the need to stop traffic at busy intersections during rush hour, providing a serious inconvenience for many commuters who had nothing to do with the movement or the problem?[1]

The questions I received from my white community were sometimes genuine, sometimes not. At times, the questions were a way out of listening, hermeneutic devices that worked to fit unknown new experiences— experiences that they did not, or did not want to, have a language for[2]—into pre-formed, static paradigms. Specifically, I found some outsiders to be too quick to ask "what are their demands?" and then immediately feel capable of judging the efficacy of a diverse, creative, and evolving social movement on the basis of the quick fulfillment of falsely unified goals. The tactic seemed to agree with the goals but "managing the message", critiquing the manner in which the content arrives. Again, that response is common but not a good way for white people to respond in solidarity. Thankfully, BLM is nonplussed. Shanelle Matthews, public relations head for the movement explains: "There is no one right way to get free. We support divergent strategies."[3]

© The Author(s) 2019
J. C. Luttrell, *White People and Black Lives Matter*,
https://doi.org/10.1007/978-3-030-22489-9_2

Seen as public, artistic, political, and ideological, the protests drew in bystanders and media to an experience that was unfamiliar to many white people. Those protests had the effect, in some non-black people, of combatting ignorance of black experience. Alicia Garza, one of the founders of the Black Lives Matter movement, describes the movement thusly: "Black Lives Matter is an ideological and political intervention in a world where Black lives are systematically and intentionally targeted for demise. It is an affirmation of Black folks' contributions to this society, our humanity, and our resilience in the face of deadly oppression."[4] Further, Matthews describes BLM's activity as "un-anchoring narratives" from dominant social narratives created about black people and their experiences and value.[5] Framing the work of the movement as "un-anchoring narratives" places emphasis on its expressive and symbolic affects, and such emphasis is important because large-scale cultural changes are, in general, expressive and symbolic, involving a changing of people's hearts, privilege, and power, as well as laws and policies.

So, to the questions I received about BLM's methods, I gave versions of a response that pointed toward BLM's expansive, revolutionary expressivity. And still, the same people kept asking the same questions. It was as if I had not spoken, as if BLM activists had never written anything, as if the conversation never happened. My interlocutors' discourse did not incorporate any explanation; they did not move beyond the question's asking. This reaction is telling. My sense is that they conceived their skepticism about BLM's methods as part of their own empathy, a part of their convicted virtue, and it was going to stay that way. I should say, too, that my frustration from these conversations was not because my friends, family, and colleagues *disagreed* with my interpretation of the protests. I was frustrated because they did not even seem to acknowledge any new information which would constitute any such grounds of agreement or disagreement. The immobility of the dialogue reminded me of the way that epistemologies of ignorance work: when ignorance is not just a lack of knowledge, as such, it is a fiction's continual re-emerges despite rational explanations that explain which falsify it. So, these conversations confirmed, for me, that it is not merely the presence of false beliefs which form a political project of whiteness, it is the fixity of such beliefs. That white empathy makes its *doxic* appearance in the form of such skepticism, ad infinitum, shows how current forms of allyship end up being projects in service of white supremacy.

Moreover, such "empathetic" distance or indifference (an "empathy" that does not make the grade) is a portal to examining whiteness as a habit, a political project. If white empathic indifference is a predominate shape of the *doxic* response to black-led political movements that habit reveals something not about BLM or Civil Rights but about white observers. If white people like myself really want to claim empathy and solidarity with such movements, we must first come to terms with the indifference which calls itself empathy.

Of course, the entirety of BLM should not be described by white people mainly in terms of its descriptive or normative effects on white people, especially not mainly as an appeal to white empathy. Suffice it to say here, the movement has many, more specific, goals and consequences, especially because it has many different, local chapters that work in ways suited to each particular context.[6] Other more specific demands and goals include, of course and, for example: calling for more federal investigations of local law enforcement, advancing a program of police bias training, reducing arbitrary inflation of bail bonds, disrupting the school-to-prison pipeline by reducing suspensions of young black students, etc. The question I am interested in, here, though, is *how* a cross-section of communities—both white and black—can become mobilized *for* those goals, without white people appropriating the movement to be something other than a black-organized and led movement. That is, how would white solidarity with BLM be possible?

In addition, BLM activists have ample reason to be wary of entering a discussion about social movements and white empathy. In "A Black History of White Empathy", Juliet Hooker argues that such a reading of white responses to black protest is misguided, because it does not account for the angry mobs of white protesters during the 1960s, who were not only resisted to calls for empathy but actively hostile toward them (as true in the North as it is in the South).[7] For example, the gains made by the Civil Rights movement in the 1960s cannot, Hooker contests, be attributed to the morally self-congratulatory, liberal, white, northern folk on the basis of their supposed-expansive capacity for empathy. Hooker is right, as are other critical race scholars like Tommie Shelby, who are skeptical of defining any part of black movements in general in terms of white empathy, because that interpretation gives the false impression that the actual agency for social change belongs to white people, in a damaging and false "savior" complex and obscures the fact and efficacy of black solidarity. Defining black social movements as calls for white empathy also obscures black self-love and self-affirmation, acts that do not, and need not, include white people.[8]

Nevertheless, I and my white friends, family, and colleagues should try to understand the experience black people at the hands of law enforcement, so that, at the very least, we do not dismiss the movement or stand in its way. The burden of responsibility for this understanding should not fall on black activists; it falls on white people. Surely, we white people who do not consider ourselves immediately involved with the problem of police violence, that is, people who consider ourselves innocent of the harms of racial injustice (as Baldwin's describes, those "innocents who constitute the crime"[9]), do not want to see the slew of black children's bodies are lying on the street, at the hands of a system we support, and so we do not want to see the mass "die-ins" in public places. But one point is that, just as surely, Michael Brown's father could not bear to see his son lying in the middle of the street when the Ferguson police force left his body in the sun for four hours. In order to work for racial justice, white people and the dominant power structures they control and represent have to, as much as is possible, understand and empathize with Michael Brown Sr.'s experience and experiences like his.

2.2   PERSPECTIVES AGAINST "JUST EMPATHY"

Objections to the claim of empathy-within-justice typically rely on a notion of ideal justice as a kind of impartiality extracted from empathetic, holistic responses to those most affected by systemic injustice. Here, using psychologist Paul Bloom as an exemplar of this view, I critically examine anti-embodied impartiality with regard to racial justice, in particular. Then, using Adam Smith and Ray Jasper, I show an alternative idea of impartiality that does not try to suppress emotional connection and understanding across different identities but rather welcomes empathy as both a descriptive reality and a normative possibility. Smith's and Jasper's "embodied impartiality" can promote solidarity with social movements like BLM.

Bloom argues that empathy is a shoddy tool for morally navigating large-scale problems of justice, because empathy does not extend to differently looking strangers.[10] In matters of large-scale justice, procedural reason, instead of empathy, applied equally to everyone at all times without exception, should rule the day. From his research on the moral development of babies, Bloom concludes that humans have an adaptive preference to prefer the familiar, and therefore "the seeds of racism", while cultivated over time through social practices, "are there from the very start".[11] In order, then, to develop anti-racist culture and practices, Bloom says we have to trick ourselves away from biased and unreliable gut reactions, including the "natural" paths that dictate the direction *toward whom* our empathy flows.[12] It is certainly true, as I explain in Sect. 2.4 of this chapter, that socially designed programs of de-segregation can indeed make people less racist. However, in defining impartiality, Bloom sets up an antipathy between intelligence (reason) and gut reactions and appetite, of which he includes empathy and has a remarkable faith in the workings of fair procedures. For Bloom, reasonably conceived procedures do err in application (especially in the case of mandatory minimum prison sentencing), but that is the price we must pay to do the greatest good for the greatest number.[13] Because there are some sorts of decisions that "should be based on objective and fair procedures, not on who inspires the most intense emotional reaction ... part of being a good person, then, involves overriding one's compassion, not cultivating it".[14]

Ray Jasper's views form a serious contrast to Blooms'. Jasper was a black man and a former Texas death-row inmate. As he was readying himself to be executed, he wrote a letter to the public. The letter is prescient, clear-headed, and moving. I quote Jasper at length:

> *I'll only address what's on my heart. Next month, the State of Texas has resolved to kill me like some kind of rabid dog, so indirectly, I guess my intention is to use this as some type of platform because this could be by final statement on earth...*
>
> *I think 'empathy' is one of the most powerful words in this world that is expressed in all cultures. This is my underlining theme. I do not own a dictionary, so I can't give you the Oxford or Webster definition of the word, but in my own words, empathy means 'putting the shoe on the other foot.'*
>
> *Empathy: a rich man would look at a poor man, not with sympathy, feeling sorrow for the unfortunate poverty, but also not with contempt, feeling disdain for the man's poverish state, but with empathy, which means the rich man would put himself in the poor man's shoes, feel what the poor man is feeling, and understand what it is to be the poor man.*
>
> *Empathy breeds proper judgment. Sympathy breeds sorrow. Contempt breeds arrogance. Neither are proper judgments because they're based on emotions. That's why two people can look at the same situation and have totally different*

views. We all feel differently about a lot of things. Empathy gives you an inside view. It doesn't say 'if that was me ...', empathy says, 'That is me.'

What that does is it takes the emotions out of situations and forces us to be honest with ourselves. Honesty has not hidden agenda....

Again, Mr. Nolan, this is only my perspective. I'm just the hobo on the street giving away my pennies. A doctor can't look at a person and see cancer, they have to look beyond the surface. When you look at the Justice system, the Death Penalty, or anything else, it takes one to go beyond the surface. Proper diagnosis is half the cure.[15]

Jasper's definition of empathy is a philosophically sound and reasonable definition: putting the shoe on another foot, feeling what another is feeling, and getting a little bit outside of one's own identity.[16] Frantz Fanon wrote a similar description of the task of solidarity: not to see the other as myself but to be able to see *through the other's eyes.*[17] Empathy is not pity or sympathy, some leftover from Victorian ideals of charity, nor is it contempt stemming from fear of being the other's state. Neither is it merely understanding a person, in Diana Meyers' words, coldly "sizing a person up", without concurrent feeling.[18] In explaining the difference between empathy and sympathy, psychologist Brené Brown confirms Jasper's account:

Empathy is the ability to place yourself in someone else's shoes and understand relate as best as you can to how that person feels in the situation ... Sympathy is the ability to express 'culturally acceptable' condolences to another's plight ... Empathy is harder to accomplish for many reasons. We not only have to actively listen to another person's problem without judgment but then be honest with ourselves and the other person about our feelings as a listener.[19]

Jasper's and Brown's definition of empathy is consistent with, as I explain in this chapter's conclusion, Adam Smith's term for sympathy[20]: understanding another with feeling, by allowing oneself to feel along with another person, in a way that is different in degree but similar in kind.

Bloom agrees that empathy belongs in personal relationships, but he argues that empathy has little place in public life, culture, policy, and law. The first question is whether empathy is possible in the public sphere, the second is whether, normatively speaking, it belongs there. Jasper sees the law's very lack of empathy as the loci of injustice in criminal justice policy.

In contrast to Bloom, who maintains that those are living the experience might be the worst people to decide outcomes of policy related to that experience (they are biased and do not possess the distance needed for [impartial] justice), Jasper contends that understanding inmates' experience is entirely relevant to considerations of justice. Further, Jasper believes that partial understanding is possible, because empathy can indeed make inroads between class and race barriers.

Objections to the claim of empathy-within-justice are worth considering because they reveal what is at stake within the construction of certain identities. In Brown's words, empathizing and "being honest with myself as a listener" involves clearing the weeds; in other words, go through a self-reflective process of facing and come to terms with the contradiction between the real and ideal versions of myself. A parallel, collective process of coming to terms with the contradiction between real injustice and ideal justice needs to happen when "we", Americans, try to respond to the expressions of the BLM movement. That is, unlike Jones' account of Thomas Jefferson, Americans must come to terms with their own idealized national identity as fair, equal, and just, contrasted with the reality that the justice system must significantly change in order for any of those ideals to be realized.[21]

In showing how [political] reason and [personal] embodied empathy interact, Bloom has a particular idea of impartiality in mind. He writes,

> under this account, impartiality emerges as a reasoned solution to the problem of coordinating the actions of rational and self-interested beings. But empathy might play a role as well. When you take the perspective of others, it becomes clear that your desires are not special. It's not only that I don't want to be harmed, it's also that *he* doesn't want to be harmed, and *she* doesn't want to be harmed, and so one. This can support the generalization that *nobody* wants to be harmed, which can in turn support a broader prohibition against harm. *Empathy and impartiality are often mutually reinforcing: the exercise of empathy makes us realize we are not special after all, which supports the notion of impartial principles, which motivates us to continue to empathize with other people.*[22]

Bloom's idea of impartiality is an abstract construction, wherein I can reasonably conceive that all people experience harm and that harm is bad. Abstract impartiality not involve having empathy for any particular person or the concurrent emotional states that are involved in interacting with a particular other. Rather, abstract impartiality involves me using my own limited experience of suffering as a paradigm for all experiences of suffering and abstracting upward. In the end, though, I am still stuck with my own experience as the paradigm to understand harm in general.

This "reasonable" process of abstraction is not strong enough to motivate me to work for racial justice. I cannot get to Michael Brown Sr.'s experience by abstracting from my own, because, as a white person, I am not going to experience any white child of mine being shot by a police officer. Bloom would disagree: "once we have a commitment to impartial principles, this can trump self-interest."[23] It is true that, in the process of becoming an adult, I grow out of a narcissistic self-orientation where I am attending merely to the experience of my own pain and realize that other people feel pain like I do, and thus realize that it's bad that people are harmed in general. However, the problem is, I might not even believe *that harm is being done*, if I cannot believe police forces would target some populations without due cause, because I have not experienced that and probably never will. Thus, if I, a white person, use my own experience—or lack thereof—of suffering as a paradigm, I am never going to get to the point in which I can believe a black person when they tell me they were unfairly targeted by law enforcement. How, then, do I get over *that* bias? Bloom's version of reasoned impartiality does not get me across that bridge.

Jesse Prinz, too, argues on similar, but not identical, grounds as Bloom. Prinz contends that "the dark side of empathy may be intrinsic to it, and it may infect our other moral responses. Empathy is not a suitable tool for morality."[24] By "the dark side of empathy", Prinz means its tendency to favor in-group relations and contribute to bias. Juries, for instance, tend to be too retributive when they hear stories of victims, because they empathize too much with the victims' suffering, and identify with them, and then pass down sentences not proportional to the crime.[25] For Prinz, empathy is essentially selfish and "pushes partiality into prejudice".[26] While Prinz does not argue, as Bloom does, for an abstract impartiality when considering justice for distant, different, others, Prinz does advocate a cost-benefit analysis driven by emotions of concern, anger, guilt, or pleasure, rather than empathy, precisely because empathy fails to achieve the impartiality that is essential for large-scale justice.[27] Prinz contends that justice demands emotions that "carry us across seas", in other words, cosmopolitan conceptions of justice that do not only correspond to singular, narrow identities. Further, these emotions need to be motivators to action, and not, as he labels empathy, further directives to quietism. Prinz is certainly on to something here, when I think about how enervating many white people's demands are that the only form of acceptable discourse is "soft" appeals to white empathy and not strong displays of black anger. However, I am not convinced a white person like myself can get to moral outrage about racial injustice without first going to through empathy or at least overcoming my own "epistemic insensitivity".[28] Otherwise, I might be inclined to believe I understood more than I do, and act on behalf of others, instead of beside or behind them—the phenomena I describe in Chap. 4. Empathy is still an epistemic precondition to solidarity in social movements, in the way that righteous anger can come out of love.[29]

Bloom and Prinz are concerned with problems of global justice, and their characterization of empathy has roots within the stoic idea of circles of care, and the Humean insight that natural sympathy develops in the closest spaces.[30] Their paradigmatic cases are environmental disasters caused by climate change and possibilities of altruism in the face of global poverty. Their perspectives are those of the bureaucratic policy-maker, using insights of social engineering to incite the best behavior from populations of relatively well-off Westerners. For Prinz, emotions like righteous, anger, guilt, or even outrage are better motivators for action with regard to injustice because they are more practically reliable. For Bloom, impartial reason is a more reliable indicator of justice.

Bloom operates with the background assumption that impartiality is essential to [public] justice. If Bloom's abstract impartiality is necessary for large-scale justice, then, certainly, empathy, defined as "feeling-with" is misplaced in such justice. However, Bloom's argument is circular; it defines the outcome first and then deduces the processes best suited to that outcome. Bloom's desired outcome itself is erroneous, because abstract impartiality is out of place within the context of racial justice within the United States. Unbiased and emotionally detached impartiality might be the model for the sciences, but it cannot be the model for large-scale social change, or, for that matter, the goal of social movements, because no one, in the United States at least, is "unbiased" in the scientific sense, when it comes to race.[31] In terms of race and white supremacy, everyone has skin in the game. White people have an active stake in promoting ideologies that shore up their own interests.[32] A hope for an indifferent observer is impossible in the case of racial justice, because one cannot get to a just impartiality by starting from one's own experience. Further, the kind of justice which Bloom is using—impersonal, procedural reason, utilitarian calculi that remains intentionally blind to identities and context, in other words, ideal justice, too closely resembles the ideal of colorblindness, an ideal that obscures the actual context, history, and reality of racial injustice.

2.3   MANAGING EMPATHY THROUGH COLORBLINDNESS

I can respect the democratizing impulses of fairness in the [somewhat] utilitarian emphasis on reason, or righteous anger/concern or guilt, over empathy. However, regarding racial justice, the justice system remains unjust because it is *too* impersonal, that is, because many white people do not understand the experiences of people of color. The excessive legalism extracted of personal empathy serves to mask and maintain racial injustice, not to correct it. Furthermore, the evolutionary reductivism that explains away public empathy denies the possibility that people, both individually and collectively, grow and change; it relies on the premise that people and societies are static.

Again, the moments of denial of [both public and private] empathy show the stake and shape of [both personal and collective] identities. Tom Digby, in his book, *Love and War*, writes that within militaristic cultures like the United States', cultures that wage war to achieve their aims, the masculine ideal of the warrior comprises the symbolic ideal for all of society.[33] The warrior ideal is, first and foremost, a road map of ways to manage and suppress empathy. The suppression of empathy is more of a requirement for men, and empathy is seen as something weak because it is symbolically associated with women. The symbolic order is maintained through sometimes violent expressions of gender policing, where "any sign of caring about suffering is seen as feminine, not masculine, and therefore met with taunts about being a pussy, little bitch, fag, wuss, etc."[34] This formation of masculine identity works its way into the suppression of public empathy, and the denial of empathy toward those within a culture who are oppressed, in this case, black populations. The suppression of empathy is something that is managed, maintained, and enforced.

In the case of racial justice, American culture enforces the denial of empathy within one group (the white power structure) and encourages empathy within another group (people of color). This racial double standard is similar to the way in which Digby describes militaristic cultures expect men to manage and suppress their empathy, while simultaneously expecting women to over-empathize (with men, mostly). White supremacy and white innocence actively maintain the suppression of empathy *by* white people *for* people of color, at the same time that the ideals of assimilation encourage empathy *by* people of color *for* white majority culture. Indeed, the phenomena by which people of color are required to understand and know white culture, wherein that understanding does not flow back the other direction, is, as Charles Mills notes, a known theme in African-American cultural expression, including W.E.B. DuBois, who, famously, wrote of the "veil" that keeps white people from knowing the condition and heart of black people.[35,36] Consider, for instance, the necessity of "code switching" and "passing".[37] Empathy is not a luxury for communities of color; it is a survival mechanism. White people become unnerved when they interpret BLM's effect, in "de-anchoring narratives", as overturning or inverting that economy of empathy, whereby understanding only flows in one direction.

In inverting the singular direction of empathy and understanding, BLM is conveying the degree to which the U.S. criminal justice system was not, nor was ever meant to be, a completely rational cost-benefit analysis of just deserts, deterrence, or crime prevention. In other words, the criminal justice system's very procedures themselves are unjust. Even an abbreviated history of prisons in the United States shows the degree to which they were never constructed (even in the ideal form) or carried out (in the non-ideal form) on the basis of reasonable, blind procedures.[38] However, now, the ideals of colorblindness and race-neutrality mask these non-ideal realities.

As it stands, there is an empathy gap between black and white people in this country. Bloom and Prinz are right to point to the lack of empathy across races. In America, it is a descriptive fact. Hooker emphasizes: "today, race, more than any other factor, delineates the boundaries of political obligation and empathy."[39] As Brittany Cooper explains, "white people and black people in this country know very different things."[40] The empathy gap persists in white communities across classes, among the poor and the elite alike. For example, Former Supreme Court Justice John Paul Stevens writes that his biggest regret about his time on the court was his vote to uphold the death penalty because, at the time, *he did not understand* how thoroughly racial prejudice shaped the application of the death penalty.[41]

White ignorance is actively maintained by the production of memory. One (of many) examples: in *Black Reconstruction in America*, DuBois described this process by which the histories of slavery, the Civil War, and Reconstruction were all intentionally left out of primary and secondary education curriculums.[42] It is only in 2015 that the first museum on slavery in America was opened.[43] White ignorance, as Mills describes, also involved the active discrediting of black testimony: during slavery, blacks were not allowed to testify against whites, and, during Jim Crow, black testimony was harshly punished, practices which Miranda Fricker notes as the paradigmatic instance of epistemic, testimonial injustice.[44] Both before and after the civil war, slave narratives had to have white authenticators in order to be published. Mills terms this sort of self-deception, the culmination of discrediting testimony, erasing history, and promoting an ideal, as a sort of "motivated irrationality". What black people have come to see in this history, in Mills' words, is that they are not seen at all. They have also come to see how the white power structure operates, because they need that knowledge in order to survive.

Importantly, though, Mills writes, the precise mechanisms of white denial of the black experience work have changed over time. Whereas, in the past, the myth of equality was preserved by excluding African-Americans from the category of full human being/citizen/person on the basis of pseudo-[racialized] science, now the myth is kept alive by the widespread belief that the United States *has already achieved* racial equality. If racial equality has already been achieved (by, say, having a black president or celebrating the inexorable gains of the civil rights movement), the current criminal justice system *cannot* be racially biased and it *cannot* be a function of continued racial oppression and discrimination. If there are cases where procedural injustice is done, say in Texas (those southern horrors), those are the too-common exceptions and not the national rule. Therefore, it is inconceivable to see why, for instance, those Ferguson protesters were so angry. That information, that social judgment, cannot be known, and the ideal of colorblindness persists. The obscuring function of the normative focus on equality is not accidental. As Linda Martín Alcoff and Mills agree, white Americans have an active interest in "seeing the world wrongly", because they have a stake in their own group privilege. Interests produce knowledge.[45]

There is also a way in which the legacies of colonialism and slavery leave a symbolic order intact and persistently re-emerging, a symbolic order which prevents white people from seeing and affording black people full dignity. The mechanisms of these refusals are gendered, and the sentiments are complex. For instance, why does the white public continue to forget that BLM is a movement started by queer women? Why do we ignore the "Say Her Name" movement that works on behalf of women victims of police brutality?[46] Hortense Spiller's "Mama's Baby, Papa's Maybe: An American Grammar Book" speaks, in part, to these historical and gendered structural impediments to empathy. There may be, Spillers remarks, yet-to-be-understood possibilities for liberation in black womanhood and black motherhood—"'Sapphire' might rewrite after all a radically different text for a female empowerment."[47] Such a text for Spillers emerges out of, not apart from, the history of severed kinship relations under slavery. However, that empowerment has little resemblance with the various names and stories that white interpreters of black kinship relations have given black women and men. White interpreters have not seen the possibilities for liberation. Our names and narratives fixed black genders in various distortions in service of colonial mastery. That colonial and white interpreters of the so-called "negro family" have so confidently imposed narratives upon kinship relations is telling. The blind conviction of texts like the 1960s' Moynihan report—the absence of the black man as father, the oppression and bodily availability of the black woman as mother—confirms to Spillers that, as a black woman, her symbolic use to a white public is as a locus for our own identity. She writes, "My country needs me, and if I were not here, I would have to be invented."[48] Again, if we are to claim empathy, we have to come to terms with not only slavery's legacy on our own symbolic order but the sheer misplaced confidence we tend to have in our ability to understand that legacy. We cannot see movements for liberation if we first name its activists as oppressed.

Crucially, though, the only way to overcome that masking function of ideals is to face, by way of empathizing, the realities of people experiencing injustice. Both ignorance and understanding are activities and not static, unchanging ontological statuses. White Americans' ignorance of black experience is an active construction, as is their lack of empathy. Because empathy is so actively being managed and controlled, empathy must truly be a threat to the status quo. Thus, only by examining those ideals and identities is justice, by way of empathy, possible. That kind of justice is rare but not impossible.

2.4   EMPATHY AND RACIAL JUSTICE: A DIFFERENT IDEA OF IMPARTIALITY

At this point, let me re-state the basic question about the relation between empathy and racial justice, in light of the evolving shape of the inquiry: does empathy, like Jasper contends, have the power against DuBois' veil, the power to correct and overcome that actively created and maintained ignorance, that quintessential American denial, and the obscuring function of ideals?[49] Or is empathy, as Prinz and Bloom claim, basically and for the most part selfish, and racist, lacking in the capacity to project oneself into situations that have no previous correspondent beyond one's own experience and identity?

Again, the first claim here is that one *can* empathize with those who are most directly affected by injustice, implying it is possible to empathize across race. That question is mostly empirical. Psychological studies confirm both the failure of people to empathize across race, and the possibility of such empathy, especially when subjects of different races have sustained contact with one another, or, simply, when they are *asked* to imagine how others feel.[50] The contact hypothesis in particular is very well supported and very little practiced. Meaningful and sustained contact between people of different races is so rare, in fact, that, as the Public Religion Research Institute reports, 75% of white Americans have "entirely white social networks", meaning 75% of white Americans do not have any non-white friends.[51] Sadly, the homogeneity of social networks did not vary significantly across political affiliation, age, or location. Thus, it is *both* true that people fail to empathize across race, and that empathy across race *is possible*. The failures and successes in empathy are due to social conditions and not due to evolution or the nature of empathy as such.

If empathy is possible but rare, Jasper's normative claim follows: cross-racial empathy is a necessary corrective to unjust law, policy, and cultural practices. In order to make that claim, one needs an idea of justice that is unfettered by a notion of abstract impartiality. In terms of justice, a more nuanced, embodied, context-specific idea of impartiality is needed. In the language of moral theory, there must be a sort of balance between Bernard Williams' strong rejection of systematic impartiality in favor of one's own projects, identity, and integrity, and the Sidgwickian strong advocacy of the "point of view of the universe".[52] Neither position is really useful to racial justice because strong particularity can serve plain-old prejudice, as is well-established, but the strong "point of view of the universe" can serve colorblindness-masked-as-prejudice.

Adam Smith's idea of the impartial spectator is different from Bloom's idea of abstract impartiality and more useful to racial justice. Perhaps this is surprising, if one were to consider Smith only in the role of archetypal proponent of modern capitalism. Because he was interested in promoting peace in the context of a growing, increasingly multicultural society (albeit in service of promoting unfettered, global market relations), Smith is concerned to document the way human beings do indeed learn, grow, and change, and become, over time, better at making humane judgments.

Thus, Smith's ideal society is not one concerned with the suppression of empathy but the cultivation and expansion of it beyond one's own self-image.

In the *Theory of Moral Sentiments*, Smith's idea of impartiality accords with Ray Jasper's explanations. For Smith, empathy (what he calls "sympathy") is not selfish. Empathy is, in fact, the singular vehicle of *ectasis*, of getting out of oneself and one's own biases and perspectives. Smith writes,

> But though sympathy is very properly said to arise from an imaginary change of situations with the person principally concerned, yet this imaginary change is not supposed to happen to me in my own person and character, but in that of the person with whom I sympathize. When I condole with you for the loss of your only son, in order to enter into your grief, I do not consider what I, a person of such a character and profession, should suffer, if I had a son, and if that son was unfortunately to die; but I consider what I should suffer if I was really you; and I not only change circumstances, but I change persons and characters. My grief, therefore, is entirely upon your account, and not in the least upon my own. It is not, therefore, in the least selfish.[53]

Here, Smith describes the process of learning and growing. In being present with another person and inhabiting their grief, I am not only myself anymore. A change occurs within me, which enables me to begin to understand experiences that I myself did not have. My own son did not die. I was not harassed by the police. Difference exists; we are not all the same. If I were to start from my own experience and abstract outwards, as Bloom defines impartiality, I would not actually succeed in grieving with my friend. Nevertheless, for Smith, empathy allows us to bridge the myopia of our own experiences and come to grapple with the presence of suffering and loss. The relevant experience in Smith's example is not his own lack of grief but the grief of the father, the person who is suffering.

Note how similar Smith's description of empathy is with Ray Jasper's description: "Empathy gives you an inside view. It doesn't say 'if that was me …', empathy says, 'That is me'." Both Smith and Jasper are saying that empathy can do exactly what Bloom and Prinz say it most often does not: bring a person beyond their own identity and expand their horizon of knowledge and experience. Empathy does this in its *pathetic* (re: *pathos*) capacity. For Smith, the potential for *ecstasis* comes not through the senses alone and is therefore not a given of all human interaction but comes through the cultivation, over time, of imaginative projection into being another person and inhabiting their world. It comes with experience. Bloom is right, in that babies are not born empathetic to out-group members. But for Smith, part of being civilized means to become empathetic, to become an adult. One must work to be empathetic, and it is the work of a lifetime. For Smith, this work is moral progress.

To note, this account of empathy's social construction distinguishes Smith from the Humean view. To be "civilized", for Smith, is to have a finely cultivated sense of empathy so that when I grieve with a person, I do not keep a safe distance and remain emotionless. I do not think of my own harm and expand that experience into an abstraction of all people's harm. If I did so, as Brown emphasizes, I would not be helping them; I would be making them feel worse by emphasizing the distance between our relative experiences, because my friend has lost his son and I have not. Rather, I "suffer with" the other person, if only for a moment and not to the degree they are suffering but to the degree that my understanding of their experience has grown and to the degree that they could feel slightly less alone in the immensity of their own mourning. The process does not produce perfect understanding, but such perfect understanding is not required for shared mourning.

Smith promotes empathy as the basis for moral sentiments and community, and for the ideal "impartial spectator" that is to arbitrate justice in a civilized world.[54] At first glance, one could mistakenly read Smith's "impartial spectator" as Bloom's ideal of impartial reason: as an indifferent spectator, not tied to any specific identity.[55] However, for Smith, the impartial spectator evolves out of a highly cultivated sense of empathy with specific others and not a denial of any specific position whatsoever. Perhaps Smith's impartial spectator reads like a contradiction because the way one cultivates impartiality is through multiple experiences of deep and profound partiality. However, that seeming contradiction is how Amartya Sen carefully distinguishes Adam Smith's impartial spectator from Rawls' [contractarian] original position, as well as any utilitarian position: the notions of just impartiality here are very different.[56] Stephen Darwall has observed that Smith's impartial spectator takes up a second-person, and not a third-person, perspective.[57] In other words, Smith's "impartial spectator" is not the view from nowhere nor is it the view of a benevolent bureaucrat who remains intentionally blind to the *pathos* of each situation. Rather, Smith's "impartial spectator" becomes impartial precisely *by* using pathos to fully inhabit other's situations and getting outside of herself.

Indeed, there is no other way for human beings, as the kind of creatures we are, to engage in the activity of making judgments—indifference is impossible. As Fonna Forman puts the matter, "A Smithean spectator has no resource but her own lights."[58] In modern terms, I cannot deny my positionality. Qua white person, I am not an arbiter of universal reason. Rather, I am a situated person working within the context of my own [limited] understanding and the power relations that shape that ignorance and understanding. However, precisely because of this situatedness, I am both ignorant of black experience *and* there exists a possibility for under-standing. In other words, I need to be able to understand the world more accurately, from the position I am in and not another.

The function of the impartial spectator is precisely to mimic the natural sympathy of closeness with another without the obscuring function of attachment to our own identity. The impartial spectator, has, in other words, mastered the *ecstatic* function and pathos of empathy. In Smith, empathy and impartiality are not contradictory, because the impartial spectator has the cultivated ability to inhabit the position of more than one (passionate, selfish) self. Smith's impartial spectator is impartial pre-cisely *because* she has the potential to (fully and empathetically) inhabit more than one (my own and another's) position. In fact, following Brown, being honest about my own position as a listener helps me understand another's experiences. I have to be honest about the power and ignorance whiteness confers upon me in order to understand first, that I do not understand, and second, to listen. Smith's impartiality is never a fixed, determinate status, but, in the Aristotelean tradition of virtue, is sort of an ongoing activity, a way of being at work. As in friendship, one is always working to understand, in deeper, fuller, and more meaningful ways, and this work is never boring or finished.

Forman maintains that "*Different sorts of impartiality are required for different sorts of judgments*, and that the sort of impartiality achieved by Smith's impartial spectator might be effective for correcting physical and affective shortsightedness."[59] This is an important insight: depending on the specific social problem, different ideas of impartiality are required. Consider, then, the kind of judgments white folks should make after encountering claims of racial justice, as indicated by social movements like BLM. Impartiality extracted of empathy looks too much like colorblind-ness, an over-ideal form of justice that is used to maintain, and not correct, racial injustice. Holding onto that ideal means holding onto the myth of one's own national identity as just, fair, and equal, and so the very ideal of impartiality itself becomes an avenue of prejudice. White people should consider movements for racial justice through the second-person, and not the third-person, standpoint. In terms of racial justice, white Americans should, and can, empathize with the experience of those who are most directly affected by injustice. Doing so does not necessarily amplify bias. Rather, the *pathos* involved in empathy corrects the very lack of *pathos* involved in the formation of unjust laws, policies, and cultural practices in the first place.

NOTES

1. See Cindy George, "Ferguson Decision Prompts Houston Protest", *The Houston Chronicle*, November 26, 2014.
2. Miranda Fricker terms the phenomena of lacking a language for an experienced injustice "hermaneutical injustice". Miranda Fricker, *Epistemic Injustice* (Oxford: OUP, 2007).
3. Shanelle Matthews, "The Communications Goals and Strategies of Black Lives Matter", *PR Weekly*, February 10, 2016. http://www.prweek.com/article/1383011/communications-goals-strategies-black-lives-matter
4. Ibid.
5. Ibid.
6. See *Black Lives Matter*, http://blacklivesmatter.com
7. Julitet Hooker, "A Black History of White Empathy", *Telesur*, February 12, 2016. http://www.telesurtv.net/english/opinion/A-Black-History-of-White-Empathy-20160211-0011.html, accessed April 21, 2016.
8. Tommie Shelby, *Who are we Dark: The Philosophical Foundations of Black Solidarity* (Cambridge: Harvard UP, 2005).
9. Baldwin, James. *The Fire Next Time*. (NY: Vintage). p. 6.
10. Paul Bloom. *Against Empathy: The Case for Rational Compassion* (NY: Ecco, 2016). See also. Bloom, *Just Babies: The Origins of Good and Evil* (NY: Crown Publishers, 2013).
11. Ibid., 106.
12. Ibid., *Just Babies*. 130.
13. Bloom, *Against Empathy*.
14. Bloom, *Just Babies*, 47.
15. Ray Jasper, "A Letter from Ray Jasper, Who is About to be Executed", *Gawker*. March 4, 2014. http://gawker.com/a-letter-from-ray-jasper-who-is-about-to-be-executed-1536073598
16. There are more technical and discipline-specific definitions of empathy, but for the purposes of this article, I stick to this cursory, working definition.

For more complete debates, see Amy Copland, ed., *Empathy: Philosophical and Psychological Perspectives* (Oxford: Oxford UP, 2014).

17. Frantz Fanon, *Black Skin, White Masks* (New York: Grove Press, 1985) 231.
18. Diana Tietjens Meyers. *Victims' Stories and the Advancement of Human Rights* (Oxford: Oxford UP, 2016).
19. Brené Brown. "The Difference Between Sympathy and Empathy", *The Mind Unleashed*. January 12, 2015, http://themindunleashed.org/2015/01/difference-sympathy-empathy.html. See also Brown, *Acompañar: a Grounded Theory of Developing, Maintaining and Assessing Relevance in Professional Helping*, PhD dissertation, University of Houston, 2002.
20. The terms are confusing here, because Adam Smith's idea of "sympathy" is roughly synonymous with the modern understanding (including Brown's, Jasper's, and my own) of "empathy". Adam Smith, *The Theory of Moral Sentiments*, eds. D.D. Raphael and A.L. Macfie (Oxford: Oxford University Press, 1976).
21. Janine Jones, "The Impairment of Empathy in Goodwill Whites for African Americans", in George Yancy (ed.) *What White Looks Like: African American Philosophers on the Whiteness Question* (New York: Routledge, 2004).
22. Bloom, *Just Babies*. 213–214.
23. Ibid., 217.
24. Jesse Prinz. "Is Empathy Necessary for Morality?" in *Empathy: Philosophical and Psychological Perspectives*, 229.
25. See, for instance, Bryan Myers and Edith Greene. "The Prejudicial Nature of Victim Impact Statements: Implications for Capital Sentencing Policy". *Psychology, Public Policy and Law*. 10, no.7 0.2004. 492–515.
26. Jesse Prinz. "Against Empathy", *The Southern Journal of Philosophy*. No. 49, 2011. 229.
27. Ibid., 228.
28. Woomer, Lauren. "Not Caring about Convicts: A Case of Affective and Epistemic Insensitivity", paper given at the Eastern Society for Women in Philosophy Conference, Houston, TX, April 9, 2016.
29. It is outside the scope of this paper to give a full critique of Prinz' views, as the aim here is to conceive of impartiality in relation to racial justice.
30. David Hume. *Enquiry concerning Human Understanding, in Enquiries concerning Human Understanding and concerning the Principles of Morals*, ed. L. A. Selby-Bigge, 3rd ed. revised by P. H. Nidditch (Oxford: Clarendon Press, 1975).
31. For research on the pervasiveness of implicit bias, see, for instance, Mahzarin R. Banji, Anthony G. Greenwald, *Blindspot: The Hidden Biases of Good People* (New York: Delacorte Press, 2013). See also Jennifer L

Eberhardt. Phillip Atiba Goff, Valerie J Purdie. & Paul G Davies, "Seeing black: race, crime, and visual processing", *Journal of Personality and Social Psychology* 87, no. 6 (2004) pp. 876–893.

32. For a definition of white privilege, see Naomi Zack, *White Privilege and Black Rights* (Rowman and Littlefield: Lanham, MD, 2015). For a definition of white supremacy, see Christopher Lebron, *The Color of our Shame: Race and Justice in our Time* (New York: OUP, 2013).

33. Tom Digby. *Love and War: How Militarism Shapes Sexuality and Romance* (New York: Columbia, 2014).

34. Ibid.

35. Charles Mills. "White Ignorance", in *Race and Epistemologies of Ignorance*.

36. Mills, Charles. "White Ignorance", in *Race and Epistemologies of Ignorance*, eds. Shannon Sullivan, Nancy Tuana (Albany: SUNY Press, 2007) 11–38.

37. On the history of code switching and passing, see, for instance, Harris, Cheryl, "Whiteness as Property". *The Harvard Law Review* 28, no. 8 (June, 1993).

38. For a history of race and the criminal justice system, see, for instance, Douglas A Blackmon. *Slavery by Another Name* (NY: Doubleday, 2008). Also Michelle Alexander, *The New Jim Crow: Mass Incarceration in the Age of Color Blindness* (New York: The New Press, 2010).

39. Juliet Hooker. *Race and the Politics of Solidarity* (Oxford: OUP, 2009) 20.

40. Cooper, Brittany "America's Fear of Black Rage: Why Tragic NYPD Shootings are so Misunderstood", *Salon*, Dec. 24, 2014. http://www.salon.com/2014/12/24/americas_fear_of_black_rage_why_tragic_nypd_shootings_are_so_misunderstood/

41. Andrew Cohen. "Why Don't Supreme Court Justices Ever Change Their Minds *In Favor Of* The Death Penalty?" *The Atlantic*. December 10, 2013. http://www.theatlantic.com/national/archive/2013/12/why-dont-supreme-court-justices-ever-change-their-minds-in-em-favor-em-of-the-death-penalty/282100/

42. W.E.B. DuBois, *Black Reconstruction in America: 1860–1880* (Washington, DC: Free Press, 1999).

43. David Amsden. "Building the First Slave Museum in America", *The New York Times*. Feb. 26, 2015. http://www.nytimes.com/2015/03/01/magazine/building-the-first-slave-museum-in-america.html?_r=0

44. See Miranda Fricker's work on testimonial injustice, in *Epistemic Injustice*.

45. Alcoff, Linda Martín "Epistemologies of Ignorance: Three Types", in *Race and Epistemologies of Ignorance*, 49.

46. See *Say Her Name: Resisting Police Brutality Against Black Women*. Kimberlé Crenshaw, Andrea J. Ritchie, Rachel Anspach, Rachel Gilmer, and Luke Harris, eds. African American Policy Forum, Center for Intersectionality and Social Policy Studies. Jan. 252,016.

47. Hortense J. Spillers, "Mama's Baby, Papa's Maybe: An American Grammar Book", *Diacritics.*, 17:2, 80.
48. Spillers, 65.
49. Gunnar Myrdal and Sissela Bok, An *American Dilemma: The Negro Problem and Modern Democracy.* Harper and Bros. 1944.
50. For support of the contact hypothesis, see, for instance, Thomas Pettigrew and Linda Tropp. "A Meta-Analytic Test of Intergroup Contact Theory", *Journal of Personality and Social Psychology* 90, no. 5, 2006. 751: 83. See also Marilynn Brewer and Samuel Gaertner. "Toward Reduction of Prejudice: Intergroup Contact and Social Organization", *Blackwell Handbook of Social Psychology: Intergroup Processes.* eds. Rupert Brown and Samuel Gaertner. Oxford: Blackwell. 2002: 451–474; James Moody, "Race, School Integration, and Friendship Integration in America", *American Journal of Sociology* 107, no. 3 November, 2001: 679–716. For evidence that empathy can occur across racial groups, see, for instance, Andrew Todd, Galen Bodenhausen, Jennifer Richeson, Adam Galinsky, "Perspective Taking Combats Automatic Expressions of Racial Bias", *Journal of Personality and Social Psychology* 100, no. 6. June 2011. 1027–1042.
51. "Analysis: Race and Americans' Social Networks", The Public Religions Research Network, October 12, 2014. http://publicreligion.org/research/2014/08/analysis-social-network/#.VWjRxkL4vFIRace
52. Bernard Williams, *Utilitarianism: For and Against* (Cambridge: Cambridge University Press, 1973, 1985). See also Williams, *Ethics and the Limits of Philosophy* (New York: Routledge, 2011); Williams and Amartya Sen, *Utilitarianism and Beyond* (Cambridge: Cambridge University Press, 1982). Henry Sidgewick, Henry. *The Methods of Ethics,* 4th edition. London: Macmillan, 1890.
53. Smith, *Theory of Moral Sentiments,* 501–2.
54. D. D. Rafael, "The Impartial Spectator", *Essays on Adam Smith,* eds. Andrew Skinner and Thomas Wilson (Oxford: Clarendon Press, 1975) 83–99.
55. This is how Martha Nussbaum reads Smith. Martha Nussbaum, *Poetic Justice: The Literary Imagination and Public Life* (Boston: Beacon, 1994).
56. Amartya Sen, "Open and Closed Impartiality", *The Journal of Philosophy* xcix, no. 9. Sept. 2002: 445–469.
57. Stephen Darwall. *The Second-Person Standpoint: Morality, Respect and Accountability* (Cambridge: Harvard University Press, 2006) p. 46. Darwall claims that Smith invented the second-person perspective in Anglo-philosophy.
58. Fonna Forman-Barzilai, "Sympathy in Space(s): Adam Smith on Proximity", *Political Theory* 33, no. 2 April 2005. 189–217.194.
59. Ibid., 207. Italics my own.

CHAPTER 3

How White People Refuse to Understand Black Mourning

3.1   WHITE RESPONSES TO BLACK-LED POLITICAL MOURNING

That white people generally refuse to understand black experience is widely acknowledged. A theme in African-American literature work in epistemologies of ignorance shows that ignorance is not only a lack of knowledge but an actively maintained state of being which works to shield white people from complicity.[1] If white people like myself admitted that Black Lives Matter's (BLM) mass "die-ins" and the words of Mothers of the Movement were in fact intelligible, we would have to reckon with the fact that we had a hand to play in someone else's loss.[2] We will not deal with that degree of self-knowledge because, for one, we are attached to a vision of ourselves as good people.[3] So we engage in denial and defensiveness, in other words, what Alice McIntyre and Allison Bailey call "white talk".[4]

However, the fact of complicity is not itself a conclusion. The discourse of complicity is now working the same way Naomi Zack describes the language of privilege working: as another form of white quietism.[5] Admittance of complicity and/or privilege becomes one more marker to separate the "good" white people from the "bad", and we again can form identity groups on the basis of being racially enlightened without engaging in political action.[6] There is more work to be done not only in concluding *that* white people are complicit but also in knowing *how* complicity works, so that we can get out of the way of movements for racial justice.

© The Author(s) 2019
J. C. Luttrell, *White People and Black Lives Matter*,
https://doi.org/10.1007/978-3-030-22489-9_3

White people misunderstand black experience as a whole but especially we refuse to understand black mourning, because mourning is the most damning and most threatening aspect of black experience to functioning white supremacy. White people refuse to understand black mourning in many, varied ways. Here, I discuss some (not all) typical and recurrent reaction strategies.[7] The first, conservative kind of reaction is common: when seeing expressions of anger and lamentation on television from black protests in Ferguson and other cities, white people equate any displays of emotion coming from mourning as a threat, as a form of violence.[8] Thus, they feel justified in dismissing any political message that comes from such a place as irrelevant. These responses come in the form of violence or "tone-policing" and "gas-lighting": hermeneutic devices that absolve people of the responsibility to understand, empathize, or respond.

A second, liberal kind of reaction often comes from white people whose acts of sympathy themselves silence black people's agency. The kind of reaction is exemplified in artist Dana Schutz' recent work, "Open Casket" at the Whitney Museum. Schultz is a white woman who painted a representation of Emmett Till's mutilated body. Protester and artist Parker Bright blocked view of the painting, wearing a t-shirt that said, "Spectacle of Black Death." Commenting on Schutz' choice of subject, Christopher Benson, biographer of Emmett Till's mother Mamie Till-Mobley, writes, "Mrs. Till-Mobley recognized the dangers that exist in the framing and representation of black people by others who lack the cultural connection, the deeply felt pain of enforced marginalization."[9] John Jennings writes that Schutz' artwork "supplants the mother's very brave act of showing us the body".[10] Schutz said that she was inspired to paint the artwork because she was sympathetic with the Black Lives Matter movement,[11] but these kinds of good intentions, at the very least, obscure the power of Mamie Till-Mobley's own [agential, brave, complex] expression of mourning.

On the one hand, there's a grain of truth in the conservative reaction: white people are right to see expressions of mourning as a threat, not necessarily a threat of violence, but a powerful threat to supremacy nonetheless. The perilous quality of mourning is a theme of ancient literature. In Antigone and the Abrahamic tradition, mourning does indeed threaten the political establishments, to their core, because grief cannot be controlled. In these texts, mourning has an undoing function; it undoes us, personally and politically. In the book of Jeremiah, mourning is actually the precondition for the radically new life and political arrangements.[12] Nowhere is there a landscape that scares us more than grief, our own and others. Thus, the conservative protestations, in the form of actual force (police militarization) and in language (tone-policing, gas-lighting), are evidence that if an oppressive order is to be maintained, mourning must be contained. The conservative reactions acknowledge mourning's power.

The liberal reaction of cultural appropriation, exemplified in Schutz' painting, distorts black mourning in a different way. It does indeed make black death a spectacle, and in doing so, it prevents the work in what George Yancy calls "tarrying": an important process whereby whites remain open to the experience of non-whites and thereby allow for the *possibility of being touched*.[13] Part of the function of tarrying is to create a space for whites to ask themselves the question: "How does it feel to be a problem?"[14] White museum-goers and, similarly, white academics who "follow" but do not support Black Lives Matter can come to see a representation of black death as a watcher/purveyor/voyeur, "sizing up" grief, but not being present with the grieving parent. White spectators can act as "scientists" of racism's processes, in protective white coats and shore up the myth of their invulnerability, a founding myth of white supremacy in the first place. They can even be invulnerable while black protestors who make themselves vulnerable in objecting to cultural appropriation.

The conservative reaction demands an idealized, perfect victim, and the liberal reaction creates one. Both reactions are shaped by respectability politics. By obscuring Mamie Till-Mobley's agency in her choice to display and photograph the maimed body of her own son, to express her own mourning, Schutz' artwork lessens the chance that we are going to understand mourning as agential at all. We misunderstand mourning from unjust deaths as only innocent victimhood. In her book, *Victim's Stories and the Advancement of Human Rights*, Diana Meyers explains that this ideal of a perfect victim is a hindrance to an empathetic response.[15] The idealized victim usually takes one of two forms: the pathetic victim or the hero. We expect the pathetic victim to have no agency whatsoever; she must be completely helpless and under the total control of others. The heroic victim, on the other hand, can be an agent, but always in a completely virtuous and nonviolent one. She can never be in despair or undone in lament. Both of these unrealistic victims share the exacting criteria of absolute innocence. The first showing of human moral frailty is grounds for victim blaming and criminalization, which the [white] listener dispenses swiftly.

White understanding of black mourning can and should evolve from victim creating, victim blaming, and respectability politics as a whole. Mourning involves the whole range of human emotion and can be a source of agency in its victimhood. Mourning, in its nature, undoes the trappings of respectability, and therein lies its power.

3.2   CONSERVATIVE RESPONSES TO BLACK MOURNING: MILITARIZATION, GAS-LIGHTING, TONE-POLICING

Before I describe the contours of some predominate white reactions to black mourning in the United States, I need to clarify two things. First, I want to cursorily delineate grief from mourning.[16] Mourning, as David McIvor writes, can be public, political, and democratic as much as it is individual.[17] Mourning is an activity, a way of being at work, and an expression calling for recognition. Grief, on the other hand, is private. It is a state of being, more passive and more vulnerable. Grief is for family and friends. It is the immediate and uncontrollable sense of loss to which we must let go, give ourselves over, in some degree, in order to move through. Mourning is more active—it incorporates our own agency as well as merely what happens to us. Mourning expands grief's circle, as an opportunity for solidarity outside of the circle of those who feel loss' gaping hole. Mourning alters private grief into public action, in the way that Elaine Scarry describes altering the unbearable privacy of pain into communicative expressions that turn oneself inside out.[18] Black-led political demonstrations are importantly not inviting a white public into their grief; they are not, for good reason, inviting that level of exploitable vulnerability. They are, in part, attempting to uncover and change injustices through acts of public mourning.

Secondly, I want to clarify again that my aim here is not to interpret Black Lives Matter; it is to interrogate common white responses to black-led protests and expressions of mourning and injustice.[19] In that vein, I am not interpreting BLM as solely an expression of mourning or giving any fixed interpretation of BLM whatsoever. I am, however, influenced by poet Claudia Rankine's writings on the subject. In "The Condition of Black Life is One of Mourning", Rankine suggests:

> The Black Lives Matter movement can be read as an attempt to keep mourning an open dynamic in our culture because black lives exist in a state of precariousness. Mourning then bears both the vulnerability inherent in black lives and the instability regarding a future for those lives. Unlike earlier black-power movements that tried to fight or segregate for self-preservation, Black Lives Matter aligns with the dead, continues the mourning and refuses the forgetting in front of all of us. If the Rev. Martin Luther King Jr.'s civil rights movement made demands that altered the course of American lives and backed up those demands with the willingness to give up your life in service of your civil rights, with Black Lives Matter, a more internalized change is being asked for: recognition.[20]

While Rankine interprets the movement as primarily "aligning with the dead" and keeping memory alive in an environment pushing toward cultural amnesia, the movement its founders Garza and Matthews describe is rich, multiple, and not reducible to expressions of mourning. Affirmation of humanity involves joy, celebration, and multiple other modes of expression and community, in addition to mourning. Christopher Lebron, for instance, reads BLM in part through the intellectual tradition inspired by Zora Neal Hurston's work, as the activity of giving oneself respect and self-regard.[21] What I am saying here, though, is that when sectors of the white public encounter expressions of black mourning, they respond in ways indicative of traditions of white supremacy, and we should work to change those reactions.

One such conservative reaction is police militarization, a direct response and immediate response to Michael Brown's death and subsequent protests in Ferguson, Missouri.[22] Since Ferguson, BLM protests around the country have experienced degrees of exaggerated police responses.[23] In one way, militarization is a response to a perceived threat, but it also has secondary intents and effects: it signals danger to bystanders and media consumers. Regardless of the protests' degree of peacefulness, heavy police presence influences a public's perception of a protest. At any rate, militarization in some ways is the most honest and direct response to the actual threat that public displays of black mourning constitute to the survival of a racial state. It is responding to threat with force.

In their initial reaction to public, creative, nonviolent actions for racial justice, white people often dismiss the content of such protests by gas-lighting the protesters. Gas-lighting is psychological manipulation that makes people question their own sanity; it is a tactic of message dismissal that pathologizes its subject.[24] For example, in August of 2014, just after Michael Brown's death, journalist Julia Ioffe interviewed white people at a Starbucks in Olivette, a predominantly white suburb of St. Louis, near Ferguson. Responses she heard on the protests include: "People are just taking the opportunity to satisfy their desire for junk", and, from a teenage boy, "It's just an excuse for people to do whatever they want to do."[25] Ioffe found that these white observers interpret any form of black-led protest as a "riot", whether or not looting occurred or protesters maintained order. Gas-lighting makes the content of the message of racial justice easier to ignore, because white observers pathologize the protests from the start.

Tone-policing is another common, conservative response.[26] White responders may be sympathetic to the content of the message, in that they believed police departments can be systemically corrupt and unfairly target African-Americans, but they perceive BLM's tactics (or, in the case of Ferguson, the many number of spontaneous protesters and new justice-oriented organizations that sprang up at the time) as disrespectable. Tone-policing and gas-lighting are manifestations of respectability politics. In the context of this book, as I have mentioned in Chap. 1, I mean by respectability politics what the Crunk Feminist Collective means:

> A nineteenth-century term and ideology, coined in the decades after slavery, which argues that if Black people acted chaste, pious, and frugal and comported themselves properly in public, they could prove their fitness for American citizenship. Today, respectability politics are often used to police Black people for nonnormative behavior.[27]

One way in which respectability politics supports white supremacy is that if all protests are read as riots regardless of how peaceful they are, the standards of respectability will never be met and the message will never be deemed legitimate. Respectability politics presents a set of impossible standards and moving goalposts. It also discourages peaceful protests from the start, because protesters see that no matter what tactics they take, they will only be read as violent. Any "disturbance" by BLM is read as violent or potentially violent. For instance, holding up traffic is violent, defending oneself against tear gas is violent, expressing anger or lament is "violent". In the United States, protests for racial justice are unique, and different from, say, the Occupy Wall Street protests or the anti-nuclear proliferation movement in the 1980s (the largest in U.S. History), because the white public is, in large part, unable to see with any accuracy the degree of violence or peacefulness.[28] A white public is inclined to read them as violent from their outset.

In describing the white responses to Ferguson, Ioffe continues: "A major problem with the protests—and they very clearly did not mean the militarized police response to the protests—was that they were tarnishing St. Louis's image as a *nice place*. 'I'm embarrassed to say I'm from St. Louis'", two women agreed. Tone-policing often works as an appeal to post-racialism.[29] Commonly, white observers will refer to their [incomplete] understanding of Martin Luther King Jr. and the Civil Rights movement and say either that BLM's framework of identity politics is incongruent with the colorblind vision they [incorrectly] learned from MLK or to appeal to [what they understand as] peaceful and nonthreatening tactics of the Civil Rights.[30] For example, journalist Isolde Raferty documents a series of private emails elementary school parents sent to a predominantly rich, white school district in Seattle after the district sponsored a "Black Lives Matter Day", in which teachers and students wore BLM t-shirts and encouraged a curriculum directed to topics of mass incarceration and racial justice. One parent wrote: "Can you please address … why skin color is so important? I remember a guy that had a dream. Do you remember that too? I doubt it. Please show me the content of your character if you do."[31]

Rod Dreher, the conservative activist and blogger who incited the right-wing threats to philosopher Tommie Curry, is another example of the tone-policing demand for post-racialism. Dreher says he is bothered by Curry's writings because they do not live up the post-racial world toward which [he perceived] MLK to have been working.[32] Dreher says he admires the children of Sharonda-Coleman Singleton, one of the black parishioners executed by Dylan Roof in Charleston's AME Church, who said that they had already forgiven Dylan Roof. Dreher's words are infuriating, and they are typical. On the way to carving out what could be a reasonable objection to retributive violence, Dreher defines "respectable" ways for others to mourn. The conservative white response, like the one Dreher gives, feels justified in mandating the boundaries of acceptable mourning. Lest it need be said, regardless of what one believes about forgiveness, whether or not Singleton's children forgive their mother's murderer is not an acceptable judgment call for white observers to make. Further, Dreher's response, and responses like his, demands people see the world through a post-racial lens, even in the face of current racially motivated hate crimes. It is a way to cover over violence even as it is happening, a way to say "you are not seeing what you are seeing".

3.3   LIBERAL RESPONSES TO BLACK MOURNING: VOYEURISM AND APPROPRIATION

White conservative and liberal responses to black grief respond dialectically to each other; they do not adequately respond to black loss. During the "Black Lives Matter" day at Seattle schools, another parent of a Latino child lamented how the day had gone for her son. She said her son had felt scared going into the day.

"After school, she learned that her 5-year-old was asked to stand up in front of his class and talk about Black Lives Matter and his shirt. By the end of the day, he had taken it off and shoved it in his cubby. I asked him why, and he said because he was tired of people asking him about it and wanting to take his picture," the mom wrote. "I was so angry all I could do was pick him up, hug him so tightly and said, 'I can see why you chose not to wear it. That sounds uncomfortable and unfair.'"[33]

In "White Allies and the American Tradition of Consuming Black Grief", Myles E. Johnson writes about how, in attending BLM protests, he experienced them in their sadness and felt vulnerable and exposed trying to negotiate public expressions of grief while being corralled by the police.[34] Johnson explains that he was, in some ways, ready for the sadness and its police suppression, but what he was not ready for was these expressions of grief being "captured" to such an extent by white voyeurs. He writes:

> What was new for me, however, was the lens in my face. A snapshot was taken of me, a White journalist recording my confused grief. The *click* of the camera caused me to look around at who else was marching with me—we were all grieving Black people. The one White person in this crowd of protesters was there to capture this funeral, not participate. To my side, on the sidewalks, were White people with apologetic signs that read "White silence is White violence." I couldn't tell if they were truly there to participate or to consume Black grief in a more thrilling, intimate way.[35]

Johnson continues, explaining how white voyeurism of black grief harkens to the tradition of public lynching, a spectacle meant to thrill the white audiences, terrify the black audiences, and confirm white supremacy.

I, and many of my liberal white colleagues and friends, "follow" and "analyze" BLM, often on social media, among ourselves. Many of us agree that BLM's demands are sound ones. To prove we agree, and to distinguish ourselves from our conservative white friends and family who do not agree, we re-post traumatic videos of police killings on social media. These postings shore up our own identity as "allies", in comparison with other white people who we confirm are not as "woke" as we are. We watch and discuss protesters' courage, action, and trauma, while not taking any meaningful risks ourselves. In our observance of black mourning, we do not make ourselves vulnerable. Such a move is not accidental. Invulnerability is one of the founding myths of white supremacy itself. As Alison Bailey writes, "Colonial master narratives have universally constructed white

selves as civilized, competent, strong, autonomous, self-sufficient, independent, pure, and stable. These narratives mythically equate white bodies, whitely habits, and power with invulnerability."[36] According to Bailey,
we forget that we too are embodied, fragile beings, capable of moving
from a state of immense joy to brokenness in grief, in a moment. Falsely
envisioning ourselves as self-contained and even slightly immortal, when
observing black mourning, we turn what could be a subject-to-subject
dialogue into an interaction where an invulnerable subject is observing a
vulnerable object.

In contrast to such a subject-object interaction, Diana Meyers takes the
death of a friend's child to be the paradigmatic moment for conceiving what
empathy looks like.[37] The occasion is heuristic, because it uncovers how
absolutely insufficient and inappropriate "sizing up" one's friend's grief is,
in place of real empathy. "Sizing up" is a cognitive understanding of another's state without concurrent feeling of one's own. It leaves the grieving
person more alone in their grief. At the worse, it compounds the trauma, in
the least leaves the grieving party wishing they had not opened up. White
liberal voyeurism amounts to "sizing up". In Meyers' explanation, "sizing
up" can resemble the indifference of pure observation.[38] It fails to be empathetic because one can try to understand a person for any number of nefari-
ous purposes, as a torturer tries to get into the head of his victim, understand
their interests, in order to be a more effective torturer. One could try to
understand a person out of detached curiosity out of what "makes her tick".
The activity of "sizing up" is one I think liberal white people are used to,
because many of us, academics or technocrats, are committed to a vision of
ourselves as expert "sizer-uppers". We get paid to explain things to people,
so we feel ourselves capable of comprehending racial justice movements
without being involved. Empathy, in contrast, involves the precondition of
caring about the other person first. In empathizing, one is not dwelling
"on" the other's state of mind, but in a limited and imperfect capacity,
dwelling "in" and with them. Thus, empathy involves sustained interaction.
Such sustained interaction can be accomplished in a number of ways, friendship being one of them but also temporarily suspending judgment in listening to or reading others' stories. Judgments can be appropriate eventually,
but empathy requires *first* caring about another person *before* making judgments. It does not make judgments in order to allow for caring.

Appropriation is another, common liberal response to black grief.
Because we—white people like myself—admire the courage, existential
risk, and agency in some expressions of black grief (and joy, and all other

feelings expressed in movements for racial justice), we often feel justified in representing it accurately. Cultural appropriation can be critiqued in all of its manifest forms—music, culture, etc.—but Schutz' painting is a salient example of appropriation of black grief, specifically. The other reason I focus here on Schutz' painting as explanatory is because I see myself in Schutz. We are from roughly the same class and place, the suburbs of Detroit, and I find myself suspect to engaging in the same kind of appropriation that she does. My deliberations on Schutz, here, then, are in some aspects self-reflection.

Schutz writes that she could not have painted "Open Casket" before she herself was a mother, imagining what she might have felt had her young child been killed in the way Emmett Till was killed.[39] Schutz explained her own work as an act of empathy. But it does not quite make that grade. Jennings is right; Schutz's own act of painting and displaying a representation of Till displaces the agential act of Till's mother, Mamie Till-Mobley.

As Mrs. Till-Mobley herself describes, she did something very hard and immensely admirable: she found power in her vulnerability and grief. She writes:

> You see, my story is more than the story of a lynching. It is more than the story of how, with God's guidance, I made a commitment to rip the covers off Mississippi, USA—revealing to the world the horrible face of race hatred. It is more than the story of how I took the privacy of my own grief and turned it into a public issue, a political issue, one which set in motion the dynamic force that led ultimately to a generation of social and legal progress for this country. My story is more than all of that. It is the story of how I was able to pull myself back from the brink of desolation, and turn my life around by digging deep within my soul to pull hope from despair, joy from anguish, forgiveness from anger, love from hate.[40]

Mrs. Till-Mobley's action involved risk and sacrifice. She describes her story as a sort of labor—a turning, digging, pulling of joy from anguish. She explains that she wrote her story, in part, so that her audience could understand how that labor occurred. She wants to help other parents who have lost children to hate crimes. Also, she makes clear that she wrote her story so that people could understand her son, Emmett, "as the driven, industrious, clever boy that he was at the age of fourteen. Forever fourteen."[41] Reading Benson's biography, in Mrs. Till-Mobley's words, allows for the possibility of "tarrying", being touched. It invites the reader into a sort of turning. Specifically, the work invites the readers to care not only about what *happened to* Emmett and Mrs. Till-Mobley, but more than that, to care about them, who they were as people.

There is so much more to be said about Mrs. Till-Mobely's act and life's activism, but I do not feel it is my place, here, as a white person, to give her work and decisions a fixed interpretation, a "last word" so to speak. First, I do not need to—she explains herself generously. I do, however, want to encourage a turning, the "worth my time" attitude toward Till-Mobley's work and interpretation. Schutz' work, I fear, does not encourage that sort of turning. By Schutz supplanting Till-Mobley's action, conduiting herself as the mother figure, we no longer see Till-Mobley in the forefront; she fades back into our imaginations as only a victim. Her story becomes uni-dimensional—not only a story about a lynching and racism but also a story about a brave woman finding meaning from suffering.

In Till-Mobley's own story, she does not present herself as a helpless victim, even though she was certainly victimized. Her account encourages an understanding of how grief and agency can work together. In the act of displaying her son's body, as Rankine interprets, she placed both herself and her son's corpse in positions of refusal relative to the expected etiquette of grief, and in doing so, "she 'dis-identified' with the tradition of the lynched figure left out in public view as a warning to the black community, thereby using the lynching tradition against itself."[42] Rankine is suggesting that Mrs. Till-Mobley turned the direction of lynching terror back at itself, at the perpetrators and not the victims and undermined its logic. Schutz' painting, in contrast, displays only "those southern horrors", far away. Are they Schutz' own horrors? We do not know. As a white woman, her (and my) identity is closer to Emmett Till's accuser, Caroline Bryant in Tallahatchie County, than to Mrs. Till-Mobley.[43] In conduiting oneself as the brave hero of this story rather than one of its villains, we white ladies not only miss an opportunity to understand how grief and agency work together, a revelation in itself, we also miss the opportunity to ask ourselves, "what forces spurred a white woman to support white men's racist violence? Are we subject to the same forces? If so, how? What can we do to keep ourselves from lying in the same way Bryant lied and from absolving ourselves the way she did?"

Art can do things beyond the artist's intention.[44] Just because Schutz characterizes her work as empathetic, she need not be taken as its most reliable narrator. I do not say this to impugn her character—I say this to show a pattern of white appropriation that I myself, and other liberal observers of black-led protest, tend to repeat. The strongest defense of Schutz' appropriation is that Schutz is a white artist talking to a white art world, reframing an iconic image from an earlier time to unsettle the myth of post-racialism in our current era.[45] Under this argument, Schutz needs to appropriate black grief to deal with white liberal "grief" that the United States is not as far along the arc of moral universe as we thought we were when we elected Obama. That move, however, still domesticates the revolutionary power of Mrs. Till-Mobley's own story. It centers white liberal feelings and story, a sort of naïve surprise at how racism still works, over the outline of black mourning. The experience of white liberal political shock is not the same experience as losing a child.

In appropriating black mourning, white people un-implicate ourselves. White appropriation of black mourning is another form of appeal to white innocence by way of virtue signaling. In contrast, Christopher Benson, Till-Mobley's biographer, calls white readers to respond to the story by letting their own innocence die.[46] The paradox is that, in observing and appropriating black grief, many liberal white observers believe they have given up their innocence. They have admitted privilege, white guilt, or complicity. But virtue signaling by way of admitting white guilt is not helpful to the goals of racial justice movements. The goal is not that white people tend to admit complicity; it is for us to stop being complicit.

3.4   RECOGNIZING AGENCY, GIVING UP THE IDEALIZED VICTIM

The perspective that sees Mrs. Till-Mobley or the Mothers of the Movement as victims without agency perspective misunderstands victimization. Diana Meyers outlines this misunderstanding in *Victim's Stories and Human Rights*. Meyers is worried about two dominant paradigms of victimhood impeding our understanding of victims' stories and action on behalf of justice. We tend to see victims, Meyers writes, as either totally pathetic or completely heroic. The pathetic victim must be utterly helpless in the face of forces completely beyond her control, subjected to unspeakable suffering. The heroic victim has agency, but must express that agency with super-human virtues, always acting nonviolently and never expressing despair or agony. These paradigms which demand the "super-humanity of some, and the evacuated humanity of others"[47], "encode polarized conceptions of innocence that are out of keeping with well-established social practices regarding the acknowledgement of victims. Worse, they block recognition of certain victims of human rights abuses."[48] These paradigms are also covers for respectability politics; they lay the groundwork for victim blaming. The listener carries around the criteria of absolute innocence to decode the "real" victims from the interlopers, and the criteria works as a tool of dismissal. The heroic, pathetic victim lens encourages judging before caring. Meyers suggests that these paradigms be replaced by a more reasonable and realistic conception of agency, the capacity for intelligent choice and action, where victims are given space for the full range of human emotions—joy, courage, celebration, hope, anger, grief, lament, and agony—sometimes at the same time, in the same person.

Within our own family and friend groups, we already empathize with those who have (a) been victimized, but are not (b) completely innocent in the sense of not having made their own decisions, however limited their decision range. Furthermore, we usually do not employ the tropes of absolute victim or superhero among our own family members; we know them too well. We can see and accept our family as complex and contradictory human beings, with a set of ambiguous emotions, like our own. Often, we respect and admire those closest to us because of these complexities, not in spite of them. The failure to apply the same skill of accepting ambiguity across identity groups is one way in which racism works. Still, there is another step a white lens typically takes in viewing black victimhood: we turn victims into criminals. If victims do not meet the stringent demands Meyer's lays out, victim blaming turns to criminalization. Alisa Bierria makes this point when analyzing Marissa Alexander's legal treatment. Marisa Alexander, a black woman and a domestic violence victim in Florida, fired a warning shot for her husband to leave the house during a violent episode.[49] In 2012, she was convicted and sentenced to a mandatory 20 years in prison. The judge in that case argued that if Alexander had been angry enough to fire a warning shot, she could not have been genuinely afraid, and thus any kind of self-defense argument was irrelevant; she was not a victim, even though her husband had admitted he had tried to kill her in the past. Alexander responded that she could be angry and afraid at the same time. The prosecution would not allow her that kind of moral and emotional complexity and so accused a domestic violence victim of being its perpetrator.

At any rate, the white conservative responses to black grief demand a perfect victim, and the liberal responses create one. If such a perfect victim is impossible, black victims are criminalized. The two kinds of white reactions are talking to each other; they are not talking with BLM activists. The paradigm of pathetic victims is useful, because white liberals are virtue signaling to their conservative contacts the identity difference between the two groups. Thus, so they look for, and create, purely pathetic and/or heroic victims that would satisfy the impossible criteria of the conservative paradigm. Insisting on the paradigm of the heroic victim is, also, a way of forgetting the Civil Rights movement; as Al Frankowski explains, it is another way to insist on post-racialism.[50] We can remember civil rights heroes in the purely heroic paradigm, as paragons of nonviolent virtue. Then we can hold this standard, peremptorily, against any current BLM action, violent or not. Holding up the Civil Rights movement this way of forgetting how radical it was, in Christopher Lebron's descriptions.[51] White observers forget King's remarks on the methods of nonviolent resistance, how one of its aims was disruption, to make the white public uncomfortable, to unsettle their sense of inviolability.[52] However, the conservative responses to black grief—dismissal, fear, and threat—actually carry a grain of truth to them. Mourning is indeed a serious threat to the political and social status quo, and it is a threat to a world shaped by white supremacy. That so much energy is spent on "white talk", and so many resources on containing these protests, speaks to their potential in this regard.

3.5   MOURNING'S POTENTIAL: UNDOING THE POLITICAL ORDER IN ANTIGONE AND THE BOOK OF JEREMIAH

One reason white people often refuse to understand black mourning is because we refuse to understand mourning as such. Two ancient texts in particular give descriptions of mourning that acknowledge its power. The Abrahamic tradition gives space to mourning in the form of lament, read as a form societal critique. These ancient texts are normatively useful, in so far as I want white people to respect expressions of black mourning outside of the contradictions respectability politics and outside of our current practices of nurtured ignorance. I am hoping resources in the Abrahamic and Greek traditions can open a door for respecting "disreputable" forms of mourning and for us to be honest about mourning's power.[53]

I want to make clear first, though, that I am not interpreting BLM or other black-led protests here as a form of a Jeremiad, "a lament that reflects the continued calamities of a people as moral punishment for their societal and moral evils as it maintains hope for a brighter future".[54] There is of course of long history of African-American Jeremiad protest, but my work here is neither to place BLM in that tradition nor forego that possibility. Again, my aim here is not to interpret BLM but merely to encourage white people to (a) make space for the range of human emotions present in mourning and (b) show how some of these ancient texts acknowledged power and agency in grief. I also wonder what prevents a white public observing black mourning in social movements from the kind of catharsis spectators at the Dionysian festival experienced upon viewing tragedy and mourning together.

In *Risking Truth: Reshaping the World through Prayers of Lament*, Scott Ellington describes the book of Jeremiah as an example of lament, where the prophet must voice truth about the pain and abandonment in his relationship between himself and Yahweh and between Yahweh and the kingdoms of Jerusalem and Judah.[55] Set during the Babylonian conquest and destruction, Jeremiah warns his fellow Israelites about imminent demise if they continue to break the covenant with Yahweh by worshipping false/other Gods.[56] In his unheard warnings, Jeremiah is a little bit like the prophetess Cassandra in Aeschylus' *Agamemnon*: gifted in seeing the future but cursed not to be believed. Like Cassandra, Jeremiah does not hold back. Famously, he describes his sustained rage: "then within me there is something like a burning fire shut up in my bones" (Jer 20:7–18).[57] Both the prophet and God speaking-through-the-prophet unleash the full spectrum of anger, derision, frustration, love, and mercy, both at each other and the Israelites. Jeremiah rails at God in direct accusation of abandonment: "Why is my pain unceasing, my wound incurable, refusing to be healed? Truly, you are to me like a deceitful brook, like waters that fail" (Jer 15:18). God, His people, and the prophet rage at each other in the language of spurned lovers who have defiled their marriage vows (Jer 2:2; 3:1). Whereas the prophet of *Lamentations* stands as an intercessor between God's anger and the people, Jeremiah's loyalty to the people is capricious, and he is not above desiring vengeance. He asks Yahweh, "Do not forgive their iniquity, do not blot out their sin from your sight/Let them be tripped up before you; deal with them while you are angry" (Jer 18:23b). Jeremiah's character and emotions are complex and ambiguous, and Yahweh too vacillates between the poles of justice and mercy. The God in Jeremiah is a God of *pathos*.[58] When I read these books in undergraduate humanities courses, it often offends students' sensibilities, their sense of divine justice, to encounter a God who rages and mourns.

Jeremiah's is not a distant God. Rather He is both limited and enlivened by very human-like emotions. Ellington suggests understanding the relationship between Yahweh, Jeremiah, and the covenant people in terms of what Martin Buber calls an I-thou relationship.[59] Buber contrasts an I-thou relationship to an I-it relationship, between a detached observer and objects of her study. An I-thou relationship is one where both parties are active agents.

Most intensely, God (as spoken through the prophet) describes how He feels about his people's abandonment:

> My joy is gone, grief is upon me, my heart is sick ...
> For the hurt of my poor people I am hurt,
> I mourn, and dismay has taken hold of me ...
> O that my head were a spring of water,
> And my eyes a fountain of teas,
> So that I might weep day and night
> For the slain of my poor people! (8:18–9:10)

Here, God's lament is unending. Nor does He desire that his grief end. He wants to "weep day and night" and change the makeup of his being so that it may be possible. Ellington explains lament's necessary intensity: "Prophecy must begin with an open expression of grief in order to cut through every attempt to cover up or deny the reality of a crisis."[60] Lament's first aim is to name a society as it is—crumbling and in crisis—and not as it should be. It shouts: "the world is not right". Jeremiah decries the "lies" of the other prophets of his time "who proclaim 'peace, peace' when there is no peace" (Jer 6:14). Laments uncover and make known the true state of affairs. Laments are uncomfortable because they "explore the extreme places in our lives ... expressing a cavernous depth of suffering and need".[61]

Importantly, in this prophetic tradition, laments are also the condition of the possibility for newness. In order to build, accept, and embrace a new world, the loss of the old world must be mourned, in full. Jeremiah bemoans that the Israelites are not mourning when they should be; they are holding on to the old world, even as they are losing it. The act of mourning, then, requires risk. In admitting that the old world is on its knees, and feeling the full force of that loss, one "abandons a pretense of excuse, denial, and cover up".[62] Therefore, "such prayers will not constrain themselves to conventional, acceptable, safe language in their address to God.''[63] Lament also comes in the moments of uncertainty, when safety and security is generally most desired, "so that denial, rationalization, or a rejection of the testimony of experience may be preferable to the risk of accepting the evidence of loss at face value."[64] Importantly, to face up to the fact that one world has been lost is no guarantee another will be gained. There is no surety to survival. Mourning, in this tradition, is "stepping into the abyss", where "newness is only a possibility, never a certainty".[65] If a new world does not come, the lamenter is merely a stranger, on a path to dying in land that is not their home. However, in this tradition, newness undoubtedly cannot materialize without lament. Lament is the condition of the possibility for the unprecedented. Crucially, mourning here does not undo the political order as such—it recognizes, comes to terms with, a political order already undone. A new political order cannot be built or accepted without giving up the old.

In Sophocles' *Antigone*, in contrast to the function of lament in the Abrahamic tradition, mourning actively undoes a state. Antigone's grief undoes the order that Creon is trying to create. Or rather, to be specific, Creon's attempts to suppress Antigone's grief unravel his state. The first point this reading *Antigone* stresses is how serious a threat the suppression of mourning is to the creation and stability of the Theban state. The second is to ask, at displays of public mourning, what is holding a white public back from experiencing the sort of catharsis the spectators of the Dionysian festival experienced, upon witnessing a play like *Antigone*?

Rankine makes an explicit connection between Antigone and police brutality in Ferguson, Missouri. In Ferguson, a couple of days after Mike Brown Jr.'s death, Rankine writes:

> It almost felt Greek. Predetermined, and hopeless. And then you had all these police cars with white policemen and policewomen, just sitting inside the cars, looking out at you. It was like you were in a theater, and they were this encased audience. It made me think of Antigone ... The dead body's in the street. What do you do now?[66]

It is interesting that Rankine feels herself here, not as the audience, but as the unwilling actor, thrust into a tragedy to be watched. She feels she is expected to play out some sort of script, to be viewed by an audience averse from entering into the play. Elsewhere, Rankine writes about how the police left Michael Brown Jr.'s body on the street for four hours, long enough for a girl in the gathering crowd to take a picture of his body and show it to his mother, Lesley McSpadden, asking "isn't this your son?" The police would not allow Mrs. McSpadden to access her son's body, because they were treating it as evidence. During this period, Michael Brown Sr. asked for his son's body to be covered up; the police denied his request. Since August 2014, there have been several theatrical productions of Antigone around the United States that link its themes to BLM.

In the play, mourning must happen. Antigone must give the burial rites to her brother. Otherwise the mortal state stands against the divine order, and, as the last lines of the play stress, "reverence towards the gods must be inviolate."[67] Creon's state must bend its own firmness and authority to allow for mourning, an interaction between both kin and gods. Since Creon remains inflexible, as the seer Tiresias describes, he has "brought a sickness to this state", where the gods no longer accept prayer or offering. Too late, Tiresias advises Creon not to murder twice over. "Allow the claim of the dead; stab not the fallen; what prowess is it to slain anew?"

Creon inaugurates his reign by drawing limits around which bodies are mournable. Eteocles, who was useful to the state, may be entombed and given rites, but Polyneices' body may not.[68] In *Precarious Life: The Powers of Mourning and Violence*, Judith Butler interrogates how a state recognizes, allows, and amplifies some expressions of grief, while making other losses ungrievable. Butler asks why it is that, according to a given state's logic, some lives are mournable and other lives are not.[69] In this vein, one can see Creon's error as attempting to constrain the boundaries of mournability, to give rites to some and not to others.

In a Hegelian reading of Antigone, as Butler describes, "Antigone comes to represent kinship and its dissolution, and Creon comes to represent an emergent ethical order and state authority based on principles of universality."[70] For Butler, Antigone is, as a representative of kinship, a figure at the edge or limit of *Sittlichkeit*, the norms and rules that govern politics. She stands for the divine order and kinship orderings that ideally should both structure a state and restrict its authority, a priori.[71] Antigone claims herself to be a representative of Zeus. The rumors of the Theban people, as Creon's son Haemon report, confirm such limits to state authority.[72] Within the logic of the state's language, then, Antigone's claims are unintelligible.

In *Antigone*, I notice the imperative of mourning, the ways it normatively orders and limits the state, and the warning against its denial. I also notice that Creon, as a kind of representative of the state, does not disallow mourning as such but only grieving for certain people, in certain ways.

He tries to manage mourning to tragic ends. The fact of his management speaks to mourning's power. Paradoxically, the order he was trying to create simultaneously depended upon and was undone by his selective suppression of mourning. The Greek tradition, seen in *Antigone*, recognizes both how the management of mourning makes and unmakes a state.

David McIvor emphasizes that grief, even or especially antagonistic grief as displayed in *Antigone*, is essentially democratic. McIvor writes,

> Grief's unmanageable excess reflects a deep source of conflict that is in constant tension with the polis' desire for order. Tragedy, as a "genre in conflict" exemplified this tension because, while it took place within the context of a civic festival that aimed in part at reinforcing the boundaries of political membership, it also gave voice to the "noncivic" passion of excessive grief.[73]

The Dionysian festival gave voice to the noncivic, excessive, passionate grief in the context of a civic experience. The literary and theatrical was a necessary addition to the life of the polis, because there needs to be a voice of unordered human passions and needs within the order of the state. Crucially, though, the audience went through the experience of tragedy together. Their catharsis was a collective one. The reason that Antigone was, in fact, a tragedy, is because the Greek audience understood *both* Creon's language of state and order *and* Antigone's liminal utterances of mourning. The fact that the audience could share in the grief of both Creon and Antigone meant that both of their positions were, contra Butler, completely intelligible. That the audience could enter into both perspectives without losing the truth of the other speaks to the power and structure of tragedy in the first place. It also speaks to the necessity of cultivating the capacity to understand human complexity within the political life of the polis. The antagonistic theory of politics that has come from readings of Antigone—one of competing, completely irreconcilable interests—is an interpretation at the level of the artwork, but it does not also consider what the artwork is doing in the audience.[74] Tragedy is played out on stage, in one respect, so that it need not be played out, over and over again, in actual politics. *Antigone* calls its audience to do the work of reconciliation that its own characters could not themselves accomplish.

White people in the United States tend to respond to expressions of black mourning by claiming it is unintelligible. The claim of unintelligibility often appears in the forms of: voyeurism ("let me look longer"), appropriation ("I will explain it for you"), gas-lighting (pathologizing), tone-policing ("I cannot hear you when you say it like that"), and militarization (repression). What these forms have in common is that they are ways of managing and suppressing mourning. The maintenance of white supremacy depends upon such management of mourning, because, as we see in Sophocles, grief can unmake a state. However, in *Antigone*, it is really the management and suppression of mourning that unmakes a state.

What would happen, I wonder, if we loosened up that control and management of mourning? What would a political comportment look like if white people stayed a while, let ourselves tarry in the sadness and injustice of the killing of kids like Travyon Martin, beautiful, bright 12-year-olds like Tamir Rice? Again: can white parents mourn black children? The question persists. I do not know if, in a society like ours, controls upon mourning, its policing, *can* let up.

One response to that question comes from the Afro-pessimism tradition, which might reply that black people in the United States cannot be mourned because they are already dead.[75] The legacies of slavery—its "afterlife", in Saidiya Hartman's description—gave a civic death to black people.[76] That death is total, it comprises the ontological horizon of the black political subject because "the entire world's semantic field ... is structured by anti-black solidarity."[77] If that worldview holds, so does Spiller's description of the symbolic economy: white supremacy sees black people as always already deserving violence, loss, degradation. In such a world, liberatory black political speech really is undecipherable to a white public. The speech resembles Cassandra's more than Antigone's, a doomed voice, unconditionally resisting reconciliation with an audience primed for catharsis. Cassandra is not mourned; she was a dead from the beginning.[78]

I am not persuaded, however, that the civic death of the black political subject is such a foregone conclusion, because it has taken me too much effort to kill her. It takes not a little bit of contortion to turn my body far enough away from BLM expressions and voices not to affect me. If I am stuck in traffic with protesters all around me, I have to turn up NPR on the radio pretty loud not to hear the chanting. When I go to the mall, I have to step over quite a few bodies lying on the floor to get to Nordstrom's. I guess I should pretend I did not see the part of the "Formation" video where Beyoncé stands on top of a sinking cop car? The justifications I need to muster to avoid engagement take a fair bit of energy to integrate into my identity as a good person, and they stay rolling around in my head long after the protest is over. The exhaustion I muster is itself exhausting. That it takes so much effort to manage the flow of my empathy (even if the effort itself is habitual, expected, and generational) speaks to the fact that, on some level, I have recognized what Anna Julia Cooper called "the spark of life" in victims of white supremacy and those who act on their behalf. I know their lives matter, I must convince myself they do not.

Thus, in contrast to responding in defensive "white talk", white people should give up expectations shaped respectability politics, work through our own fear of mourning, and move toward creating the kind of public, democratic environment which holds space for complete and impolite expressions of lament and mourning, both our own and other's.

NOTES

1. See, for instance, Charles Mills, "Race and White Ignorance", in *Race and Epistemologies of Ignorance*. Shannon Sullivan, Nancy Tuana (Albany: SUNY Press, 2007) 11–38.
2. On "Mothers of the Movement", see, for instance: "Who are the Mothers of the Movement?", *International Business Review*. July 26, 2016. http://www.ibtimes.com/who-are-mothers-movement-families-police-shooting-victims-speak-day-2-dnc-2394960
3. Shannon Sullivan, *Good White People: The Problem with Middle Class Anti-Racism* (New York: Suny, 2014). Barbara Applebaum, *Being White, Being Good: White Complicity, White Moral Responsibility, and Social Justice Pedagogy* (Lanham: Lexington, 2010).
4. Allison Baily, "White Talk as a Barrier to Understanding Whiteness", in George Yancy (ed.), *White Self-Criticality beyond Anti-racism: How Does It Feel to Be a White Problem?* (Lanham: Lexington, 2014) 37–57. Alice McIntyre, *Making Meaning of Whiteness: Exploring Racial Identity with White Teachers* (Albany: State University of New York Press, 1997).
5. Naomi Zack, *White Privilege and Black Rights: The Injustice of US Racial Policing and Homicide* (New York: Rowman and Littlefield, 2015).
6. Shannon Sullivan's *Good White People* gives a thorough analysis of white construction of virtue based upon class differentials.
7. These strategies are not an exhaustive description of all possible reactions white people have to BLM. For instance, I do not discuss challenges to patriotism, individual weapon stockpiling, or sheer exhaustion at any great length. The reactions I chose to discuss are ones I which, as I see it, tend to be assumed reasonable enough to be publicly justifiable.
8. See, for instance, Brittany Cooper, "America's Fear of Black Rage: Why Tragic NYPD Shootings are so Misunderstood", *Salon*. Dec. 24, 2014. http://www.salon.com/2014/12/24/americas_fear_of_black_rage_why_tragic_nypd_shootings_are_so_misunderstood/

9. Christopher Benson, "The Image of Emmett Till", *The New York Times*, March 28, 2017. https://www.nytimes.com/2017/03/28/opinion/the-image-of-emmett-till.html

10. John Jennings, as quoted in Benson, "The Image of Emmett Till."

11. Calvin Tomkins, "Why Dana Schutz Painted Emmett Till", *The New Yorker*. April 10, 2017.

12. Inspiration for this line of inquiry came from Cheyney Ryan, "The Dilemma of Cosmopolitan Soldiering", *Heroism and the Changing Character of War*. Sibylle Scheipers (ed). (London: Palgrave Macmillan, 2014) 137.

13. George Yancy, "Tarrying Together", *Educational Philosophy and Theory*, 2015. 47:1. 26–35.

14. George Yancy, *Look a White! Philosophical Essays on Whiteness* (Philadelphia: Temple UP, 2012) 16.

15. Dana Tiejens Meyers, *Victims' Stories and the Advancement of Human Rights* (Oxford: Oxford UP, 2016).

16. I thank Alfred Frankowski for this insight. The political difference between grief and mourning is important and fruitful theoretical ground. The cursory definition I give it here will not suffice to give proper credit to the distinction's profundity. However, as my focus here is how white people refuse to understand black mourning, and not the distinction itself, I leave that work aside in this chapter.

17. David McIvor, *Mourning in America: Race and the Politics of Loss* (Ithaca: Cornell UP, 2016).

18. Elaine Scarry, The Body in Pain: The Making and Unmaking of the World (Oxford: Oxford UP, 1987).

19. For full interpretations of BLM, see Keeanga-Yamahtta Taylor's *From #BlackLivesMatter to Black Liberation* (Chicago: Haymarket, 2016). Taylor specifically clarifies the differences, tensions, and solidarities between BLM the organization and BLM the movement.

20. Claudia Rankine, "The Condition of Black Lives is One of Mourning", *The New York Times*, June 22, 2015. https://www.nytimes.com/2015/06/22/magazine/the-condition-of-black-life-is-one-of-mourning.html

21. Lebron, *The Making of Black Lives Matter*, 57.

22. see American Civil Liberties Union (ACLU) Report: *War Comes Home: The Excessive Militarization of American Policing*. June 2014. https://www.aclu.org/sites/default/files/field_document/jus14-warcomeshome-text-rel1.pdf

23. In *#From BlackLivesMatter to Black Liberation*, Taylor documents how the groundswell of protests in Ferguson were not representative of BLM as an

organization, nor were the protests representative of any given organization or institution at all. 153–190.

24. Robin Stern, *The Gaslight Effect* (New York: Harmony, 2007).
25. Julia Ioffe, "What White St. Louis Thinks about Ferguson", *The New Republic*, August 14, 2014. https://newrepublic.com/article/119102/what-white-st-louis-thinks-about-ferguson
26. For this analysis on tone-policing, I am indebted to Ashton P. Woods, Black Lives Matter activist in Houston, TX.
27. Index of terms, *Crunk Feminist Collection*, Brittney C. Cooper, Susana M. Morris, and Robin M. Boylorn (eds.) (New York: The Feminist Press, 2017) 328.
28. David Courtight gives an account of the positive public response to the broad coalitions formed in the anti-nuclear protests in *Peace: A History of Movements and Ideas* (Cambridge: Cambridge UP, 2008) 126–151. Jess Zimmerman has also pointed out the discrepancy in arrests between BLM protests and the Women's March in "The Myth of the Well-Behaved Women's March", *The New Republic*, January 24, 2017. https://newrepublic.com/article/140065/myth-well-behaved-womens-march
29. Alfred Frankowski has described the ways post-racialism works as a vehicle for forgetting and neglect. See *The Post-Racial Limits of Memorialization: Toward a Political Sense of Mourning* (Lanham: Lexington, 2015).
30. Cristopher Lebron and Penial E. Joseph rightly correct the notion that the Civil Rights movement was respectable in the manner this liberal response is describing. See Lebron, *The Making of Black Lives Matter*, and Joseph, *Waiting 'Til the Midnight Hour: A Narrative History of Black Power in America* (New York: Holt, 2007).
31. Isolde Raferty, "To Understand White Liberal Racism, Read these Private Emails", KUOW, June 16, 2017. http://kuow.org/post/understand-white-liberal-racism-read-these-private-emails
32. Steve Kolowich. "Who is Left to Defend Tommy Curry?" *The Chronicle of Higher Education*, July 26, 2017. http://www.chronicle.com/article/Who-s-Left-to-Defend-Tommy/240757
33. Ibid.
34. Myles E. Johnson, "White Allies and the American Tradition of Consuming Black Grief", *The Establishment*. Aug. 16, 2016. https://theestablishment.co/white-allies-and-the-american-tradition-of-consuming-black-grief-5050567dc779
35. Ibid.
36. Alison Bailey, "White Talk", 50.
37. Diana Tietjens Meyers, *Subjection and Subjectivity: Psychoanalytic Feminism, and Moral Philosophy* (New York: Routledge, 1994).

38. Meyers, *Victim's Stories and Human Rights* (Oxford: Oxford UP, 2016) 148.

39. Caitlin Gibson, "A White Artist Responds to Outcry over her Controversial Emmett Till Painting," *Washington Post*, March 23, 2017.

40. Mamie Till-Mobley and Christopher Benson, *Death of Innocence: The Story of the Hate Crime that Changed America* (New York: Random House, 2004) xxii.

41. Till-Mobley, *Death of Innocence*, xxiii.

42. Rankine, "The Condition of Black Life is One of Mourning."

43. Lorena Muñoz-Alonso, *Artnet News*, March 21, 2017. https://news.artnet.com/art-world/dana-schutz-painting-emmett-till-whitney-biennial-protest-897929

44. There is an aesthetic theory functioning in the background of my account here, but it outside the scope of this chapter to work out such a theory in any systemic sense. That the artist's intent does not constitute the entirety of the art works' meaning must suffice as an axiom, in this chapter, rather than worked-out conclusion. I do not give a systemic aesthetic theory here because my analysis of Schutz' painting is not a cornerstone to a theory of political whiteness—it is only one type, among others, of common reaction to black-led protest. To claim that there is meaning beyond the author's intention is not to say, like extreme post-structuralists, that the meaning lies wholly in the audience' hands. I only want to say that if activists like Parker Bright claim "Open Casket" is doing more harm than Schutz' interpretation of her own work would convey, it is worth white people's time to tarry with Bright's contentions, given the epistemic privilege his situation confers within the nexus of race relations in the United States. Beyond that, the debate about artist's intention is huge, spanning analytic aesthetics to literary theory. For an extreme and historically paradigmatic versions of these views (and ones I do not wholly share), see Monroe Beardsley and William K. Wimsatt, "The Intentional Fallacy" (1946) in Joseph Margolis, ed., *Philosophy Looks at the Arts*, 3rd edition, 1987. See also, Roland Barthes's "The Death of the Author", 1967.

45. I am indebted to Ashley Hope for this insight.

46. Christopher Benson, *Death of Innocence*, preface.

47. Meyers, *Victim's Stories*, 53.

48. Ibid., 18.

49. Alisa Bierria, Free Marissa Now Coalition, News Release, November 24, 2017.

50. Frankowski, *The Post-Racial Limits of Memorialization*.

51. Lebron, *The Making of Black Lives Matter*.

52. Martin Luther King, Jr. "The Other America". 1967. Stanford University.

53. The sources from which I draw here—Jeremiah and Antigone—are importantly not the only ancient sources which give political meaning to mourning. For instance, Aeschylus' Cassandra presents a figure who, unlike Antigone, operates at the limit of the state and whose speech may actually be unintelligible within the world of the state's symbolic meaning. Alternately, there is a wealth of resources in the book of Job on purported "friends", well-wishers, who fail to adequately respond to Job's grief. I do not write on either of these figures here, but I think there is fertile ground in both to expand a political theory of mourning.

54. Willie J. Harrell, *Origins of the African-American Jeremiad: The Rhetorical Strategies of Social Protest and Activism, 1760–1861* (Jefferson: McFarland, 2011) 7.

55. Scott A. Ellington, *Risking Truth: Reshaping the World Through Prayers of Lament.* Princeton Theological Monograph Series (Eugene: Pickwick, 2008). Kindle edition.

56. Ibid., location 1228.

57. Charles Blow, in fact, names his memoir *Fire Shut Up in my Bones*, recalling the prophetic tradition here (Boston: Houghton Mifflin Harcourt, 2014).

58. Walter Brueggemann, "The Costly Loss of Lament", *Journal for the Study of the Old Testament.* 36 (1986) 57–71.

59. Ellington, location 533. See Martin Buber, *I and Thou.* Walter Kaufman, trans. (New York: Scribner, 1970).

60. Ellington, 995.

61. Ibid., 666.

62. Ibid., 169.

63. Ibid., 171.

64. Ibid.,78.

65. Ibid., 95.

66. Meara Sharma, "Claudia Rankine on Blackness as the Second Person", *Guernica*, November 17, 2014. https://www.guernicamag.com/blackness-as-the-second-person/

67. Sophocles, *Antigone*, RC Jebb, trans. http://classics.mit.edu/Sophocles/antigone.html

68. Of Polyneices, Creon decrees: "none shall grace him with sepulture or lament, but leave him unburied, a corpse for birds and dogs to eat, a ghastly sight of shame."

69. Judith Butler, *Precarious Life: The Powers of Mourning and Violence.* NY: Verso. 2006. Also *Frames of War: When is Life Grievable?* (NY: Verso. 2016).

70. Butler, *Antigone's Claim: Kinship Between Life and Death* (New York: Columbia, 2000) 3.

71. When Creon asks Antigone whether she knew she was transgressing his edict in burying her brother, she responds: "It was not Zeus who had

published me that edict; not such are the laws set among men by the justice who dwells with the gods below..."

72. The "murmurings" and "moanings of the city for this maiden" are that "no woman ever merited doom less—none ever was to dies so shamefully for deeds so glorious as hers."

73. McIvor, *Mourning in America*, 43.

74. On the agonistic model of the political, see Chantal Mouffe, *On the Political* (New York: Routledge, 2005).

75. Afro-Pessimism's concept of the civic death of the black political subject comes out of Orlando Patterson's book *Slavery and Social Death* (Cambridge: Harvard, 1985). Afro-Pessimists argue that white supremacy fixes black subjects in this social death, extending Patterson's description of slavery to a world order shaped by anti-blackness. See Jared Sexton, "Afro-Pessimism: The Unclear Word", Rhizomes, Issue 29, 2016. William David Hart argues for this perspective as related to Trayvon Martin, in "Dead Black Man, Just Walking" in *Pursuing Trayvon Martin: Historical Contexts and Contemporary Manifestations of Racial Dynamics*, Janine Jones and George Yancy, eds. (Langham: Lexington, 2012).

76. Saidiya Hartman, *Lose Your Mother: A Journey Along the Atlantic Slave Route* (New York: Farrar, Straus and Giroux. 2008).

77. Sexton, 58.

78. On Cassandra, See Alfred Frankowski, *The Post-Racial Limits of Memorialization: Toward a Political Sense of Mourning*. New York: Lexington. 2015. Also, there are conversations happening between Afro-Pessimist perspectives and BLM, both in scholarly settings and in activist spaces (re: Sexton). I do not need to interpret those conversations here, because they are conversations about the efficacy and strategies of activism, which, as I explain in Chap. 4, as best left to activists themselves.

CHAPTER 4

Respecting Black Lives Matter as Political Action

4.1   How Political Action Is Different
from Scientific Inquiry

Expanding on the second chapter's concept of impartiality, this chapter applies parts of Hannah Arendt's idea of political action to BLM activists. Then, in part because of Arendt's own blind spots regarding black-led social movements in her own time, I read political action through James Baldwin's idea of public love and encourage white people to take up Baldwin's map of a visionary moral conscience, which includes accepting our own vulnerability and mortality.

For Arendt, political action, as opposed to work or labor, is the precondition for the radically new, and its outcomes are unpredictable, because action is the site of creating meaning and freedom. Social movements like BLM are essentially different from science or policy measurement in the way that, for Arendt, the social realm was distinct from the political realm. Of course, social movements call for important policy interventions, but the methods of such calls—the creative action that brings about policy change—have a different nature than the policy prescriptions themselves.

Organizing and activism is a unique sort of activity; it changes and reveals a person's character. In the process of organizing, individuals and groups are learning new things at each step and initiate yet-untested political organizations. The process is one of informed improvisation, and there is little element of "predict and control" that characterize the scientific or policy realm. Participation in social movements more closely resembles

J. C. Luttrell, *White People and Black Lives Matter*,
https://doi.org/10.1007/978-3-030-22489-9_4

community action planning, wherein action, reflection, and information gathering happen simultaneously.[1]

Thus, white people who are not involved BLM, but who feel themselves capable of predicting its efficacy, are misunderstanding the nature of social movements, especially movements for racial justice. The third-person perspective, the objectivity of the so-called "view from nowhere" we can believe ourselves to possess is appropriate in other contexts, like scientific inquiry and, in some cases, policy intervention. But such a perspective is not appropriate in predicting the outcome of black-led social movements. Expertise on social movements comes from being involved in them. As such, BLM is not immune from judgment and criticism. It is only that those who are on the ground and doing the work are qualified to give such criticism; they have epistemic privilege. It is the first person that is most relevant in this context.

Perhaps because we white people often assume a false position of invulnerability, we often feel ourselves able to objectively critique black-led social movements. As have mentioned repeatedly, one common white liberal line is to critique BLM activists' methods but not their goals. In doing so, the white liberal's mostly unscientific bias masks itself in the language of social science. For instance, a common position might be articulated like, "I agree that there should be greater accountability in police forces, but I do not think that stopping traffic on a busy intersection is the most effective." Or, "Why are BLM activists organizing at the mall, when, if their object is the police, they should be organizing at police stations?" Or, "Until they have a unified goal, they are not forming a coherent public address." This posture of critique, where any white observer, whether knowledgeable or not, can feel themselves the expert, misunderstands the kind of objectivity which is appropriate to social movements. The critique is, firstly, a red herring, because critiquing the movement's form is another tactic of dismissal, a way to feel better justified in not listening and responding to its content. Given that liberal white people might be the target audience of certain protests,[2] critiquing the form of protests based on perceived effectiveness can be a way, in Jones' terms, of goodwill whites not giving the protest the "time of day", that is, not stopping, listening, engaging, and responding.

Detached, third-person objectivity may be more appropriate in the sciences,[3] but a different kind of impartiality is, as I have argued in Chap. 2, needed for social movements and most especially for movements for racial justice in the United States. Social movements are not lab tests; they are not controllable, replicable, or easily demarcated into variables.[4] On the one hand, in Chap. 3 I discussed how white critiques of black-led social movements are often fraught because our interpretive lens is itself sullied and bent. For example, if all protests, violent or peaceful, are read as violent from the outset, self-reflection about the accuracy of the interpretation must occur before a sound critique can be given. However, more than the relative inaccuracy of the interpretive lens that comes with the empathy gap between races in the United States, there is another, broader point here about social movements in general: the predict-and-control stance of social science, even good social science is out of place in the context of social movements like BLM, because they are, in Hannah Arendt's sense of the word, unprecedented political action.

Of course, most of the time the said social-scientific model that white people apply to BLM is less than scientific. Most reflection about BLM comes from amateurs, wherein nonexperts can hold forth about matters that require training. These observers do not realize the depth of knowledge that comes with a history in political organizing. Of course, in some ways, when it comes to public organizing, nonexpert opinion is expected and encouraged. Such is the democratic nature of social movements, where all citizens are invited to participate. Thankfully, one does not need an advanced degree to have a political opinion and to engage in democratic social movements. Still, expertise in social movements' tactics does exist, and just because everyone is invited to participate does not mean, ipso facto, that everyone is an expert before participating. Strategic expertise comes along the way, in the activity itself.

However, besides the common, amateur criticism, the outsider's social-scientific posture of critique is also replicated in scholarship and political theory. For instance, at the end of *Mourning in America: Race and the Politics of Loss*, David McIvor advises Black Lives Matter activists on how to empower their mourning for political purposes, given his own insightful theory of recognition and Greek tragedy.[5] In another instance, the authors of the *Journal of Political Philosophy*'s symposium on Black Lives Matter interpret freestanding claims of racial injustice without engaging with the voices of BLM activists themselves.[6] That error is partially understandable given the institutional pressure for the humanities to replicate the methods and terminology of the social sciences, to gain credibility and rigor in a science and technology-driven value system. However, a different kind of rigor, one of commitment, participation, and relationships, must be the standard in evaluating social movements like BLM.

Before yoking political movements to Arendt's theory of action, I want to clarify my claim's limited scope. The argument is not that white people should never critique BLM's tactics, because objectivity is, ipso facto, impossible from an outsider's perspective. Nor am I arguing that social-scientific lenses are not, in many cases, very useful to determining the effectiveness of social movements. I am, however, urging skepticism regarding outsiders' predictive claims about the movement's strategies and humility on the part those who feel empowered to make such predictions. White people who express skepticism about BLM's revolutionary power based of strategic critiques misunderstand the nature of social movements as unprecedented political action.

On the first point regarding an outsider's objectivity in political judgment, it is indeed possible to agree with the goals, but not methods, in a movement in which I myself do not participate. There can be soundness in such a position: For instance, I generally support People for the Ethical Treatment of Animals' (PETA) goals of reducing cruelty to animals, but I do not condone pouring blood on unsuspecting people to achieve those ends. Such a position is cogent. I am not out of line in critiquing PETA's methods, because, firstly, my critique is a moral/deontological one, not empirical, and I do not purport to have knowledge I do not have. In other words, I have no idea about whether pouring blood on movie stars wearing fur is effective in reducing overall rates of animal cruelty. But even if it is effective, my critique would still stand, because I do not think wearing animals warrants public humiliation in a moral sense. Similarly, if I am a pacifist, I can soundly critique any group that might use violence to support human rights and say their ends do not justify their means. The white, liberal, technocratic critique of BLM is different, however. It is not moral and/or deontological. Few would say it is *wrong* to hold up traffic or kneel for an anthem as such, perhaps because we would sound too much like the conservatives with whom we do not share an identity category. Rather, our objective is disingenuous. We mask our annoyance at inconvenience, or our decision not to give the protests "the time of day", in nonmoral language—consequentialist-sounding false concern—and say that they are not *effective* or *efficient* enough.

Secondly, social-scientific approaches are indeed appropriate to measuring some of the goals and demands of social movements, and one need not be an activist to do such measurement. There are many, varied goals of BLM, and it is entirely possible to measure such goals as, for instance, whether body cameras or racial bias training reduces the rate of police shootings or whether a certain program in racial bias training reduces police escalation. However, it impossible for the outsider to *predict* whether certain collective political actions, like boycotts, protests, campaigns, will shift the culture and institutions enough to accomplish BLM's concrete, measurable goals. The impact of collective action may become visible only after the fact, and still more impacts are visible to activists themselves. Furthermore, the language that best describes such impacts will be, in addition to social-scientific language, a broader, humanistic discourse on metaphysical recognition and the expression of the full range of human experience and emotion. Because social movements' effectiveness rests upon widespread cultural shifts, the language of "hearts and minds" is entirely applicable here. The outcomes of movements for racial justice are not predictable in advance, because the freedom and meaning that comes from them is brought about in and through their actors' struggles. As Keeanga-Yamahtta Taylor writes of BLM, "Justice is not a natural part of the lifecycle of the United States, nor is it a product of evolution; it is always the outcome of struggle."[7]

4.2   Political Action as Unprecedented

In *The Human Condition*, Arendt distinguishes three fundamental human activities: labor, work, and action. In her estimation, the modern world has lost a sense of how to value political action and has reduced political action to behavior, a category of human activity which is observable and predictable in the social-scientific model. If everyone is always behaving, and never acting, human activity is not free. When modern world confuses action for work and labor, it fails to act politically. That loss is lamentable, because political action is, for Arendt, the only activity where people experience and create freedom and meaning. It is the most human of all activities. Political action is fundamentally different from behavior, because its purpose is originative and revelatory. Political action has the possibility of creating new social arrangements, new "worlds", as it were, and breaking radically from past trends and cycles. In public speech, political action can make claims about justice, for instance, and bring about radically different histories and patterns. In its originative and creative capacity, political action was, in Arendt's language, the realm of natality, of birthing the new. The social sciences are the wrong tool, then, to account for political action, because they could only observe behavior confirmed and accounted for the world already in existence.

Since BLM's goal is to replace new and just social formations and do away with old, unjust ones, social science cannot predict whether it will succeed. The world the movement is trying to bring about has the character of the *unprecedented*. There has never been a context, like in the United States, where there occurred a collectively reckoning with the history of slavery and a demand of such a radical reckoning, and turning, from that history of oppression. The social-science model observes and predicts, based on past and current empirical evidence, rightly so. But to frame social movements *solely* within the realm of social science misses their important work and unique character: they create *new* social histories, reveal the character of the people involved, and actively create meaning and freedom. If we consider BLM as political action, then a notion of knowledge-in-doing emerges, and we afford epistemic credibility to the activists themselves, who have been shaped and changed by their own social struggle.

For Arendt, political action is speech in public. Action can only occur in the company of other people; it is not found in the space of individual contemplation. It involves risk, in front of and with others. Political action sets new courses of history in motion. It is a beginning. She likens action to a birth, where a completely unprecedented person arrives on the earth, someone no one has seen or met before, special and unique, and is thus a herald of hope. There is no determination that this new person will repeat the mistakes of her parents or grandparents, nor inflict the same traumas. Such a person or action embodies a hope that the old ways do not have automatic control over the future, and therefore, in shifting the weights of history, there is a hope for freedom. Action, like a child, makes known that a different future than the one currently being experienced is possible. Arendt writes "To act, in its most general sense, means to take an initiative, to begin ... to set something in motion."[8] Political action, contra social science's predictive aim, is essentially unpredictable.

Action comes from a part of the human being that is absolutely distinct from her interests and rationality, in the economic sense. The social-scientific posture does not leave enough space for newness.

Arendt continues:

> The new always happens against the overwhelming odds of statistical laws and their probability, which for all practical, everyday purposes amounts to certainty; the new therefore always appears in the guise of a miracle. The fact that man is capable of action means that the unexpected can be expected

from him, that he is able to perform what is infinitely improbable. And this again is possible only because each man is unique, so that with each birth something uniquely new comes into the world. With respect to this somebody who is unique it can be truly said that nobody was there before. If action as beginning corresponds to the fact of birth, if it is the actualization of the human condition of natality, then speech corresponds to the fact of distinctness and is the actualization of the human condition of plurality, that is, of living as a distinct and unique being among equals.[9]

When Arendt speaks of new histories occurring under the guise of a miracle, describing it as "startling unexpectedness", I recall James Baldwin, when he writes that what he is asking for—in part, white self-recognition—is impossible. "But in our time, as in every time, the impossible is the least that one can demand—and one is, after all, emboldened by the spectacle of human history in general, and American Negro history in particular, for it testifies to nothing less than the perpetual achievement of the impossible."[10] Baldwin may have the daring to "ask for the impossible" because he is a witness to black-led social movements which did indeed set new histories in motion. If BLM is doing something similar, the outcomes from its activists' public speech and action cannot be predicted, in advance, by outsiders.

Taylor writes of the formation of BLM as a moment of "rupture", a breakthrough in the segregated silence around the racialized experience of law enforcement. She explains, "As the United States celebrates various fiftieth anniversaries of the Black freedom struggles of the 1960s, the truth about the racism and brutality of the police has broken through the veil of segregation that has shrouded it from public view."[11] There were, according to Taylor, other periodic ruptures—the beating of Rodney King, for example—and even though they did not lead to a movement like BLM, they were not forgotten. The language of rupture Taylor uses to describe BLM gives it the character of the unprecedented. This is not to say that BLM has no precedents or no past. Taylor is careful to emphasize that the Rodney King beatings were a precedent, as was Ella Baker's 1950s civil rights organizing (I will speak more on Ella Baker later in this chapter), along with black nationalist and prison abolitionist movements. BLM is connected in very meaningful ways to the history of black-led organizing in the United States, both in terms of the civil rights movement and black power and black feminist movements.[12] Describing BLM as a "rupture", however, in part implies that, just as mid-century whites could not predict the revolutionary outcomes of Civil Rights movement at its time,[13] so the potential revolutionary outcomes of BLM are not wholly visible to us now.

BLM is unprecedented in another way. Taylor is careful to distinguish BLM from Civil Rights in a few, important ways: first, BLM is intersectional, led by women, and decentralized. By intersectional, Taylor means that the BLM activists start from the recognition that oppression is multidimensional and must be fought on different fronts.[14] For instance, BLM activists were not only advocating accountability for police but also rewriting a media narrative that criminalized African-American victims or promoted BLM activists (themselves) as terrorists.[15] In contrast, Taylor writes that "mainstream civil rights organizations tend to focus on legalistic approaches to resolve police brutality, compared to [BLM] activists who connect Police oppression to other social crises in Black Communities."[16] That BLM's activists see its goals as comprehensive rather than limited in scope is not as an accidental failing but an intentional strength. A legalistic approach which focuses *only* on, say, bail reform, while not also focusing on education on how a system of mass incarceration is the latest iteration of Jim Crow laws, does not make the kind of comprehensive cultural change for which BLM is calling. Taylor also describes BLM as intentionally decentralized, creating organizing spaces in the model of early Students Nonviolent Coordinating Committee (SNCC) organizer Ella Baker, where the movement is less personality-driven and hierarchical and more localized and democratic.

During and after the Ferguson protests, many different organizations and relationships came together, both local and national. Some institutions were well established, like the churches that housed the organizers, and some, like Hands up United and Campaign Zero, were forming on the spot.[17] Organizers considered collaboration between different, disperse groups a strength and did not see the need to fold organizations on one another for the sake of unity. Finally, as Taylor stresses, BLM is a movement led, in many ways, by women, in contrast, the common story of the Civil Rights movement was a movement led by men who made decisions behind the scenes.[18] So BLM already has, I would argue, the character of the unprecedented, both in its breach with past patterns of silence around racially segregated experiences and in its break from patriarchal and respectability-politics-driven organizing strategies.

Again, BLM is a "break", a "rupture" with past, confining patterns from the past, and this break both reveals the freedom of the activists to make their own way and creates a future-looking freedom that recognizes the future is not necessarily subject to the seemingly over-determined patterns of the past. Arendt's paradigmatic example of action's natality, in its freedom-revealing and freedom-making capacities, is forgiveness.[19] Forgiveness is the most "action"-like reaction, because it "is the only reaction which does not merely re-act but acts anew and unexpectedly, unconditioned by the act which provoked it and therefore freeing from its consequences both the one who forgives and the one who is forgiven".[20] Forgiveness is a freedom-making act, because freedom, in this sense, is independence from a chain of causality. The reaction most appropriate, and predictable, to transgression is vengeance. There is an automatic and cyclical character to vengeance and a never-ending, foreseeable response. Forgiveness, in contrast, arrives on the scene as unexpected, improbable, even miraculous.[21] If forgiveness is political action's exemplar, vengeance is action's contrary. If one cares to create a new world, one does not repeat the grudging patterns of the old.

I must note that, if we were to read the Civil Rights movement as political action, Nussbaum's assurances that King's speech was steering his audience away from vengeance would seem redundant.[22] Kings audience of political actors were, like BLM, trying to create a new world of justice, and therefore were not primarily or only concerned with vengeance, or merely reversing the direction of the old world of domination and humiliation that white America had inflicted upon them.[23] A white public that could only see vengeance in King's incitement to revolution could not see civil rights' participants as political *actors*, out to break the chain of violence and create something new. The white imagination saw King's audience merely as re-enacting a pattern of *behavior*, as if it were the black audience who were, in Baldwin's words, "trapped in a history they don't understand". But again, if white people read vengeance on those faces, they were seeing themselves.

At any rate, as much as action is about natality, it is also about mortality. For Arendt, as the only mortals in an immortal universe of regenerative nature and eternal gods, action is the most human of activities, because it is the only way for humans to be immortal. Action sets histories in motion that last beyond a singular lifespan.[24] In this way, both people and history are "birthed" in the activity of political action. When I think about action's relation to mortality, I am also reminded of Claudia Rankine's characterization of BLM as mourning and remembrance. There must be an important difference, then, between vengeance and mourning's respective relation to the past. In some traditions, mourning, as I have outlined in

Chap. 3, must be accomplished before a new world can be welcomed. Even though, in remembering the dead, it is oriented toward the past, mourning is also future oriented in a specific way. In the case of BLM, mourning very literally calls for a new future where people do not die in the same way at the hands of an unjust system. Vengeance, in contrast, re-enacts the old world. BLM makes mourning a political action.

When Patrisse Khan-Cullors, one of the three founders of BLM, organized one of its first protests in Beverly Hills, she described the meaning of her communal action thusly:

> And with a bullhorn in hand … I say that they, those who have come for brunch, have to confront the police presence today but that this is our everyday. I say that we were not born to bury our children, we were born to love and nurture them just like they were, and because of this, finally we had to acknowledge that in fact this is what we had been forced to do and we had been forced to do it for too long, for centuries too long. We say that those children, now our dead, now our Ancestors, are calling to us, Trayvon is calling to us and asking that we remember so that we at last make the change that deserves to be made, that has to be made. I ask the people who are lunching, perhaps spending more on a single lunch than many of us spend to feed our families for an entire week, to remember the dead and to remember that once they were alive and that their lives mattered. They mattered then and they matter now.[25]

When Khan-Cullors says of Trayvon Martin and others killed at the hands of the law that "their lives mattered then and their lives matter now", she points to a particular relation to the past that the dead do matter in the present. Remembering the dead is one and the same act of calling for change in the future. Khan-Cullors does not make a distinction between the two.

4.3   POLITICAL ACTION AS REVELATORY

In addition to being unprecedented, political action is also revelatory. Action, for Arendt, shows "who" a person is, versus "what" they are, i.e., what qualities, talents, and shortcomings they possess. The public space of action, the polis, is the space of appearances where I appear to others and others appear to me.[26] This appearance can only happen in a common space; I cannot appear in private, alone, in isolation. Because, for Arendt as for Aristotle, the human being was first and foremost a social creature, this space of appearances can only occur among others. Action establishes and alters human relationships.

The memoirs and personal accounts of BLM shore up, in some ways, the revelatory characteristic of political action. In her book, *When They Call You a Terrorist: A Black Lives Matter Memoir*, Khan-Cullors writes about the process in her own life that led up to her founding the movement, along with Alicia Garza and Opal Tometi. Much of the memoir is dedicated to Khan-Cullors' older brother, Monti. Khan-Cullors grew up watching her brothers' early adolescence be shaped by the repetitive visits from police, where they were rounded up and beaten only for hanging out together in an alleyway. She reflects on the code of silence around her brothers' experience. In their home, they did not process the steady police shakedowns after the fact. Eventually, the occurrence just became expected and enclosed by humiliation and a code of suppression, enforced by expectations of masculinity. When Monti was later diagnosed with a mental illness, she details the horror at his experience with law enforcement, brutalizing him because of his disability. These experiences function as the foreground to her leadership in BLM. When she hears about Mike Brown's killing in Ferguson, she writes, "it could always have been my brother left there on the street for hours, not only killed by a cop, but dishonored by a force of them."[27]

That she chose to record the movement in the form of a memoir speaks to the ways in which her leadership in the movement reveals who she is. Khan-Cullors' political actions show more than the old feminist/identity politics anthem that "the private is public, and the public is private". The very public police attitudes toward her black brothers influenced her family life in such a way that, when the police displayed the same violence with other families, she was moved to respond. She had empathy enough to use her own experience to work on behalf of others. Of course, when Arendt stressed action's revelatory character, she emphatically did not mean the merging of the public and private. Nor would she, as I will discuss, have recognized ways in which BLM activists like Khan-Cullors turn their private experience into inspiration and fuel for their public action. Yet, contra Arendt herself, I think the way Khan-Cullors foregrounded the movement as personal is precisely how political action is "revelatory", in the Arendtian sense. Khan-Cullors does not divorce her own self from her public action. At the same time, her action is certainly on behalf of more than herself, and she is not only working for her own, so-called "private" interests, in the economically "rational" sense of the word. She did not, personally, know Mike Brown or his family or the women in the #sayhername campaign that highlighted black women victims of police violence. Police violence and racial injustice is a very public issue, and Khan-Cullors does not, strictly speaking, gain personally from having a public voice in it. Nevertheless, her public speech, "with bullhorn in hand" is meant to be revelatory of who she is. She writes that she is proud of the work that she and others have done, and her own memoir of her life is, as her title speaks, "a Black Lives Matter memoir."

Arendt writes that action can only occur among people. Above all, it forms relationships. This is what she means when she says the public square is the "space of appearances" for the "who" someone is. One's self cannot appear without others to witness. Both Khan-Cullors and Taylor emphasize the importance of relationship building in the coming-to-be era of BLM. Khan-Cullors describes a process of connecting with organizers all over the country, meeting some of them for the first time in Ferguson. Khan-Cullors spends a fair amount of time detailing what it was like to meet and engage with others in the movement. She is not an organizer working alone, and she speaks to the great sense of meaning she found in connection. Khan-Cullors and Taylor describe the movement as intentionally diffuse, because it is a collaboration between so many different, local organizations. Each local organization includes its own, local voices to set the agenda best suited to each particular context. Thought of as a network and not a single organization, BLM leaders like Khan-Cullors and Garza emphasize the importance of relationship in the activism work, and relationships can only happen in a face-to-face setting. Therefore, local agenda building is important, because the local context creates the public "space of appearances" for activists' voices to matter. Local contexts give especially the space of appearance to women and young people, whose voices and roles the broader national media tend to overlook. Again, Khan-Cullors and Taylor both strongly emphasize that BLM's structure was intentionally founded in contrast to the older, more legalistic civil rights-oriented organizations; there is not one or two male, national voices that "speak for" the movement or set its agenda. There are many different actions and collections of people around the country, each responding to their own needs while also having a national conversation.

4.4   Political Action as Knowledge-Creating

Finally, BLM should be considered in the frame of Arendtian political action, because, in addition to being revelatory and unprecedented, there is a certain epistemology appropriate to black-led political movements, a knowing-in-doing, and an epistemological privileging of the political actors themselves.

The modern world, Arendt writes, has little concept of action and mistakes action for fabrication or making. The model of fabrication is one where the craftsman "sees" the model beforehand and then proceeds to carry out his vision. In fabrication, knowing and doing are separate activities. One "knows" the blueprints and then one constructs. The architect and the builder do not even need to be the same person. She writes that the division between knowing and doing, a division "alien in the realm of action", belongs more to fabrication, "Whose processes obviously fall into two parts: first, perceiving the image or shape (eidos) of the product-to-be and then organizing the means and starting the execution."[28]

Modernity, Arendt writes, misapplies this epistemological order, where knowing precedes doing, to political action, and then mistakes fabrication for political action. People fail to act, then, and so to have a space for any political action whatsoever. She attributes the origin of this mistake to Plato, the first to substitute making for action "to bestow upon the realm of human affairs the solidity inherit in work and fabrication"[29] In action, as we know, the futures that are set in motion are radically unknown. Arendt reads Plato as wanting to ascribe a certainty to political action which simply was not there because he wanted to convince his audience of the hierarchy of the philosopher-king. The republic is, in this way and others, an anti-democratic text. The Platonic vision is where a single ruler is most fit to engage in politics. It is not a world in which not many voices distinguish themselves in the political realm, among equals. The philosopher-king was more epistemically privileged because he had the "blueprints" for the just laws. He only needs to be in place to envision them; the guardians can carry them out. Yet, one can only have that certainty of predicting the future in the activity of fabrication. For instance, I can predict, with relative certainty, that the ship I am building, if I build with good products and good craftsmanship, according to natural laws, will not sink. No such certainty is available in politics, in the ever-shifting net of human relationships. Arendt writes, "In the *Republic*, the philosopher-king applies the ideas as the craftsman applies his rules and standards; he 'makes' his City as the sculptor makes a statue; and in the final Platonic work these same ideas have even become laws which need only to be executed."[30] But political action does not correspond to this epistemological order of ideal visions and perfect executions. When one shows oneself in public, one is setting in motion a process that is, crucially, outside of one's control. Because it rests upon the ever-shifting ground of human relationships, other free human beings, action's outcome depends upon others beyond oneself. Moreover, it depends not only upon others' "behavior" but others [unpredictable] political action.

BLM activists, I think, know the "unpredictability" of their political action and thus wisely respond to outcomes in an improvisational, ever-changing way. There is not, as in the Platonic model, one [male] philosopher-king, all knowing in advance about the laws that he needs the rest of society merely to implement and not also to form along the way. The Ella Baker model of political organizing and mobilizing here is important, a model which again, as Khan-Cullors, Taylor, and Pandit emphasize, is central to BLM's broad vision. Ella Baker was an early founder and organizer of the Student Nonviolent Coordinating Committee (SNCC) from the 1950s onward. Her goal for political organizing was to empower people themselves to be organizers and leaders, rather than for a single person to embody the grand vision and have his underlings carry it out. She described her goals as, "organizing people to be self-sufficient rather than to be dependent upon the charismatic leader."[31] As Charles Payne writes of Baker, "From her perspective, the very idea of leading people to freedom is a contradiction in terms. Freedom requires that people be able to analyze their own social position and understand their collective ability to do something without relying on leaders."[32] Like John Stuart Mill's theory of liberty in self-rule, if the goal of political movement was indeed freedom, hierarchical interventions into people's own freedom-making activities is a self-defeating contradiction in terms.[33] Thus, Baker emphasized a model of "group-centered leadership" over "leader-centered groups" that moved away from centralization and bureaucracy. The group-centered leadership had to be small and local enough for people to form meaningful relationships within them. Baker felt that when the groups got too large, certain voices, especially those from rural and lower-income communities, tend to be drowned out and replaced by media stars who lose commitment to the people in a pursuit of external recognition. Baker was especially impressed by the cell structure of the communist party, where small groups met regularly and maintained strong relational bonds among themselves, while retaining contact with other cells in other geographic locations. This way, if a large-scale mobilization was necessary, as in Ferguson, Missouri, around Mike Brown's death, coordinated action could occur.[34] The small groups were especially important to emphasize the voices of women and young people, people who, according to Baker, most often end up doing what needs to be done and not just giving orders, along with lower-income and rural community members. Payne writes of early the SNCC organization under Baker's guidance that "Its scale helped make that community possible, just as it helped each member of the organization to feel that his or her contribution mattered."[35] Community, in other words, was the space of appearance for the political action of its members. In giving each member the appropriate space for their contribution to matter, participants reveal themselves, what issues were important to them and what was at stake. Before building relationships, this knowledge about people's own revelations could not possibly occur. Thus, the only epistemological model appropriate to these communities was one of knowing-in-doing, not the fabrication model of knowing everything beforehand and executing afterwards. It is impossible to know what's on people hearts before listening to them.

Crucially, Baker had a vision of what a successful organizing might look like: it was one where the organizers learn things, if they build relationships, if they themselves become more empowered. Payne recounts:

> How many people show up for a rally may matter less than how much the people who organize the rally learn from doing so. If the attempt to organize the rally taught them anything about the mechanics of organizing, if the mere act of trying caused them to grow in self-confidence, if the organizers developed stronger bonds among themselves from striving together, then the rally may have been a success even if no one showed up.[36]

If the organizers learned something, there would be something to celebrate. What they would learn, they could not know beforehand. They learned it along the way, in trial-and-error. "Growing in confidence", too, is a way to describe a freedom-making activity. If the organizers grow in confidence in their ability to work together to break the causal chains of domination, there is something to celebrate.

The BLM/Ella Baker and Arendtian action epistemological model of knowing-in-doing, what could be otherwise called knowing-along-the-way (or knowing-in-participation, ground-up knowledge, non-hierarchical knowledge, etc.) corresponds very closely to the epistemological model of community action planning (CAP). CAP is a field of international development study and practice that advocates that "practical and strategic work go in parallel, not in sequence."[37] It encourages development practitioners (international NGOs and organizations like the United Nations, for example) to engage in small actions with local participants as a way of building relationships and then reflect on the efficacy of those actions in accordance with a broader vision, built together between international and local actors. CAP draws from the work of Don Schon's *Knowing-in-Action*, who writes, "Usually, we think this way: 'Good practice derives from good research, which then informs good policy. We now know that this is hopeful at best. Instead, I argue, *good practice derives from good practice*—where principles, methods and ideas can be tested, documented and constantly modified based on progressive reflection and learning.'"[38]

What the community action planners mean by knowing-in-action is in contradiction to the typical development pattern: doing extensive research to come up with maps of stakeholders and policy prescriptions, that is, understanding *before* action, and then leaving the "action" segment up to local stakeholders who had minimal input in the "expert" process of policy analysis. CAP tends to distain methods which involved a single comprehensive evaluation of all options, usually by a master planner or corporate developer who alone defined the objectives.[39] Instead, the first action community action planners take should give information about the next action and the broader goals. For the so-called "experts", as with local stakeholders, learning happens along the way, within the context of community and relationship building. Planners make relationships with many different members of the community, specifically highlighting the input of women and young people. Oftentimes, relationship building happens in unique and creative contexts. For instance, CAPers might ask children to create artworks or stage a puppet show to express what they care about in their own community. Or they might try to hang around for a while in public spaces like hair salons to markets to try to talk to women who were not on the list of "acceptable" cultural translators. Women and children's voices, as Ella Baker knew, may not be so loud in larger, patriarchal spaces, so personal relationships become the most effective avenue of hearing them. Because new information appears along the way, CAP recognizes the value of improvisation, spontaneity, and incrementalism. Lindblom calls this approach "the science of muddling through".

Nabeel Hamdi writes that CAP's emphasis on knowing-in-doing is so crucial, in part because it counters the prevailing, international-development narrative that the "experts", like the UN or global NGOs, have an almost unreal gift of knowing. These experts might work "on the ground" for a short period of time, trying to implement strategies which change locals' "behavior" and measure their success not in terms of whether they improved people's quality of life and well-being but whether their placements helped to advance their careers.

> The result of only "top-down" thinking: "a false sense of quality in the exactness of plans and a bureaucratic dreamland of place and community. Worse still, a false sense of achievement among experts, a false sense of excellence. This 'relentless pursuit of excellence' is the expert's badge of distinction' and the trademark top-down providing. It is how we build our reputations and earn our status professionally. It is, however, an anti-social and self-deluding kind of expertise, because it breeds a false sense of self and also another kind of inequality, this time between experts and non-experts. It alienates ordinary people, and makes them feel stupid."[40]

If CAPers want to be effective, they must change their grand goals to be the sole measure of success, and work with, and not on behalf of, local stakeholders. They also must shift their epistemological expectations, gaining a sense of humility about what they can know about what is good for a community before forming relationships. These are the central tenets of community action planning, and they correspond closely to Ella Baker's and BLM's models of political organizing, as well as to Arendt's distinction between action and fabrication.

What, then, if the white imagination saw BLM as a kind of Arendtian political action? That is, what if we saw BLM's actions as unprecedented, revelatory, and in the business of creating knowledge, freedom, and meaning? Hopefully, we would be epistemically humbled enough to realize that those who participate in social movements are best suited to determine its directions and future actions. I am hoping that describing BLM as political action is one way to give the movement the respect it deserves, and encourage white democratic responses to be less judgmental, and more dialogical and engaged.

4.5   ARENDT'S FAILURE TO RESPECT BLACK-LED SOCIAL MOVEMENTS AS POLITICAL ACTION

Arendt would not have agreed that white people should respect BLM as political action. She notoriously denied the Civil Rights movement to be an example of political action. Instead, she saw much of civil rights movement, especially school desegregation, as an instance of "the rise of the social", a trend in modernity where private interests take precedence over truly public concerns.[41] I have maintained, contra Arendt, that the civil rights actors, like BLM, were and are courageous risk takers, showing themselves in a public space to create meaning and freedom. Instead, Arendt saw the black parents who sent their children to be harassed at white schools as mere social climbers and not as rights-bearers, demanding equality for their families. As Kathryn Gines closely documents, Arendt clung to her stance even when she was called out by James Baldwin and Ralph Ellison, who pointed out that she misunderstood their writings and the movement more broadly.[42] Arendt, Gines argues, had no excuse. She did not research the subjects of school segregation scrupulously enough to realize that her interpretations, even about basic facts about geography and location, were inaccurate.[43] Her failure to research was not merely an oversight. She did not feel her subjects were worth researching. She did not think it worth her time nor did her white publishers or audience. Her failure to even read her critics positions her as another liberal "well-wisher"—a well-wishing that turns out to be a narcissism.[44]

Most condemning, Arendt did not, as other intellectuals of her time like Gunnar Myrdal and Richard Wright, see anti-black racism as a white problem. She saw anti-black racism as a negro problem. Such a failure to understand anti-black oppression is disappointing, because Arendt's analysis of Jewishness in her earlier writings and her own description of her own Jewish identity as "purely political"—"not social, not emotional"—could have lain a groundwork for a fruitful comparative analysis of oppression.[45] Thus, Gines concludes, "Arendt's delineation of the Negro question as a social issue prevents her from recognizing that anti-black racism {like Jew hatred} is a political phenomenon."[46]

Further, there is an ill-fated stringency to which Arendt insisted on the separation of her categories. For her, there was no room in public action for "social concerns", so much so that it is unclear what, if anything, counted as political concerns. The political's content, at the end of *The Human Condition*, remains surprisingly empty. Feminists and Philosophers of Race have extensively critiqued Arendt for denying that the private is political, which it indeed can be when it comes to, for example, reproductive health or neighborhood redlining.[47] I do not carry the degree of Arendt's categorical absoluteness nor feel the need to be all that faithful to Arendt's own intentions here. In applying BLM to Arendt's category of political action, I am doing something she herself would not have done and, what is more, would not have consented to be done. Gines contends that Arendt's absolute distinctions between the public, private, and social give her blinds spots on racial oppression in the United States.[48] I agree. So-called "private" concerns like school desegregation, the school-to-prison pipeline, police brutality, and mass incarceration are, in my estimation, entirely relevant in the public realm.

Another objection to the claim of activists' epistemic privilege is that Arendt explicitly defines judgment as Kantian disinterestedness and liberation from one's private interests. Judgment then becomes a concept that looks very much like social-scientific objectivity or the stock account of impartiality. She distinguishes judgment from understanding, where one "feels at home", and bemoans that the modern world has lost the capacity for judgment.[49] Gines is skeptical of Arendt's claim of objectivity, of right to judgment, regarding school desegregation without concurrent understanding. When Arendt interprets the photographs of school desegregation in Little Rock and Charlotte, she, in Gines words, "is not seeking understanding, she thinks she already understands. Arendt looks upon the photograph with already formed assumptions that adversely impact how she sees and judges them."[50] That is, when reading moments in the Civil Rights movement, Arendt replicates one of the most intractable and problematic aspects of whiteness, the posture of invulnerability in assumed objectivity.[51] Without her earlier writings on Jewishness, one could very easily read Arendt's account of judgment as a wholesale condemnation of identity politics and situated knowledge.

Given the challenges of ushering Arendt to view black-led political movements, namely, her own blind spots, what's left of Arendt's notion of action if not her strict distinctions and praise of disinterestedness? What stands is her critique of the social sciences and the powerful attributes she ascribes to public action. What is useful here in Arendt is her worry about the mis-application of a social-scientific outlook to all realms of human activity, a mis-application that constrains human freedom and meaning.

So, Arendt's description of political action is useful in giving BLM its due, but only up to a point. Given her own immovability regarding her interpretation of Civil Rights in her own time, a defense of BLM must take leave of Arendt at some point. Arendtian philosophical recovery stops at the point of her own work's narcissism, her refusal to care about black-led movements and scholars. Her correspondence and reading of James Baldwin make the location of that point of departure transparent. Firstly, Baldwin's interpretation of the black-led political movements of his era— black nationalism and civil rights among them—is undoubtedly more understanding and accurate than Arendt's. But more than a diagnostic of his own time, Baldwin's political philosophy on love is a visionary moral conscience for white people.

4.6   BALDWIN ON POLITICAL LOVE

Responding to Baldwin's essay, "Down at the Cross—Letter from a Region in my Mind",[52] Arendt wrongly interpreted Baldwin as proposing a "gospel of love", and argued, true to form, that love did not belong in the public, political realm. Arendt's interpretation of Baldwin was reductive. Along with mediations between his youth in the church and adult encounters with the Nation of Islam, meditations on mortality, freedom, and meaning, the essay reflects upon the necessity and concurrent difficulty of love in an era of anti-black oppression. By love, Baldwin means something very different from Arendt, who defined it as purely private affection. Baldwin's love was public daring and risk.

He emphasizes that there a fair number of white people who "know better" than to believe black people are inferior to white men, but "they find it very difficult to act on what they know" because "to act is to be committed, and to be committed is to be in danger."[53] Further, he locates the onus of responsibility for loving squarely on white Americans, as first self-love. That is, white people loving themselves is a form of public risk. He writes that it is a serious misunderstanding of white people to think that they have the love that black people desire or need. Rather, he is encouraging white people to learn how to love themselves and each other, which means, in part, learning to risk and be vulnerable.

> There appears to be a vast amount of confusion on this point, but I do not know many Negroes who are eager to be "accepted" by white people, still less to be loved by them; they, the blacks, simply don't wish to be beaten over the head by the whites every instant of our brief passage on this planet. White people in this country will have quite enough to do in learning how

to accept and love themselves and each other, and when they have achieved this—which will not be tomorrow and may very well be never—the Negro problem will no longer exist, for it will no longer be needed.

Baldwin is just enough of an existentialist to give clues about what loving and accepting oneself might mean, for white people. Part of that effort is accepting our own vulnerability and mortality, instead of projecting our darkest fears onto black populations. Love, directed at oneself, is facing one's own death. He writes, "It seems to me that one ought to rejoice in the *fact* of death—ought to decide, indeed, to *earn* one's death by confronting with passion the conundrum of life ... But white Americans do not believe in death, and this is why the darkness of my skin so intimidates them."[54] We earn our deaths by being fully present in what he will later call the "sensuality" of the present moment, the loving of breaking bread together, and being fully present with one another.[55] It is because white Americans do not believe in death that we are so intimated by what we believe black people represent.

The denial of mortality in whiteness is a colonial inheritance. Other people's flesh is wounded, humiliated, and decays; not our own. We must prove this by wounding others, symbolically and literally trafficking in black people's flesh. The more I outsource all my exposure and weakness to black people, the less I need to expose myself. There is extreme cultural pressure on white people, and I think especially white men, to deny and curse their own weakness. Vulnerability, emotional or physical, is teleologically directed toward death. So the denial of vulnerability is the denial of death. However, the colonial mask of invulnerability was always a mirage. It laid death upon colonial subjects, where colonists could ignore, for a while, their own fragility through acquisition of power. But it becomes impossible to mourn, let alone support the mourning of another, if one does not believe in death in the first place, one's own most of all. If BLM is in some sense about mourning, white people must first confront our own mortality—and learn to love ourselves through it—before we can claim to support a political movement of mortal remembrance.

Arendt says that the political realm is the space of appearances for mortality, but I think that Baldwin understands that point in more wisdom. In theorizing a public realm where love has no place, even if it is where humans appear as they are, in their spontaneity and natality, the political subject's mortality remains a vague simulacrum, an ideal. Baldwin is right: love and mortality show up together. It is not possible for a human to come to terms with our mortality without love and the risk of losing it. And so, if the political realm is the space of appearances for our mortality, so it must be the space of appearances for love.

The way Baldwin gives proper credence to the relationship between love and mortality reminds me, of all people, of St. Augustine, in the passages from the *Confessions* where he describes the loss of his close friend whom he loved as if he were immortal.[56] When Augustine's friend died, he realized for the first time, painfully, that those we love the most perish. Young Augustine felt the pain of the loss in his body; he could not eat or sleep and the daily pleasures he once enjoyed no longer held any joy. Augustine's extreme suffering prompted him, ultimately, to hedge his bets and direct his love only to an eternal God, who could never be lost. Clearly, Baldwin does not turn to loving God over and against loving people in the world, but Augustine's episode does point to the realization that mortality and love appear on the scene together. Concurrently, love is not possible without death.

For mature people, or parents, the fear of losing a loved one or a child is greater than the fear of losing oneself. Maturity is, I think, in part, learning to love another so much that you let go of putting first the order of importance of one's own death. My fear of death was stronger when I was single. Now, having a son, the dread that comes when I think about what it would be like to lose him—or have to leave him—is much greater than when I remember episodes in my life where I have almost died. But the thing is, white people are not mature. Thus, for us, mortality's dread is centered squarely in the direction of the loss of self, including the loss of our own identity. To dis-identify with whiteness' contents (anti-blackness) can feel like, to white people, a sort of death.

Again, Baldwin's model for the sensuality of being fully present in one's life—what he means by *earning* death—is breaking bread. Once, in *The Fire Next Time*, Baldwin uses the word "communion" to describe the tenor of his longed-for interaction between people. Yet this issue of communion, which to Baldwin was an issue of how we look at one another, is central to his political philosophy. His mention of communion comes when he describes his disillusionment with the church in Harlem, so the context inclines him to use religious language, but the way he uses it is not in reference to the parishioners. He is speaking about the possibility of recognition among and between races in the United States. He writes that being born black in an "anti-sexual", white country, "You very soon, without knowing it, give up all hope of communion."[57] He describes communion as when people look at one another, that is, when they recognize one another. Baldwin condemns the way white people *look* at black people, pass them in the street, emphasizing that liberal white people, especially, must give up seeing black people only as symbol or victim.[58] Acknowledging one another, "feeling felt", as it were, is an absolutely critical aspect to human experience. "The universe which is not merely the stars and the moon and the planets, flowers, grass, and trees but *other people*, has evolved no terms for your existence, has made no room for you, and if love will not swing wide the gates, no other power or will can."[59] So here, Baldwin posits love as a force for recognition, both between and among races. It is not, for Baldwin, any kind of guarantee, but only the (and the only) possibility for transcendence of oneself, an escape from narcissism.

I once heard the word communion defined as "beginning to understand another's prayers." I was in church, because that is where one hears these kinds of words, instead of academic translations like "recognition". A Korean–American guest pastor, Mike Whang, was recounting his experience being placed in a predominately white, suburban church in Texas after growing up in a Korean and black community in Los Angeles. He spoke about how his wife was slightly angry that he had been assigned to lead this church, in all places, and how uncomfortable he felt trying to relate to the congregation. Then, he explained, he hung around longer and started slowly forming one-on-one relationships. He said he felt more grounded when, after a while, when "began to understand their prayers". I took that he meant that he began to understand their struggles, their family turmoil, their desires, their hoped-for futures. He did not take the expected conclusion that he and the parishioners had the same life longing and desires or struggles, only that he was beginning to understand theirs. Nor did he claim full understanding. I appreciated that he used the word "beginning"—he did not demand full and total correspondence of knowledge or any such unreachable goal. Recalling Chap. 2, empathy need not demand absolute correspondence between minds to qualify as such. One does not need to be perfect to be present.

Whang's description of beginnings reminds me of one of my favorite poems: "Prayer" by Carol Ann Duffy. The third stanza of the poem starts:

> Pray for us now. Grade 1 piano scales
> console the lodger looking out across
> a Midlands town. Then dusk, and someone calls
> a child's name as though they named their loss.

Reading the poem, I like reflecting on how it is "Grade 1 piano scales", a beginner's clunking out notes, could offer consolation. And the piano scales offer consolation for no small thing—the loss of a child. The poet verges upon entreating the beginner's notes themselves to pray for her. The lines have encouraged me: we can be novices and learn to mourn with others. Beginners can offer consolation.

I related to Whang's experience. I also feel most grounded when I am in a community of people that can be vulnerable enough to share what is really going on with them, where we name the things about which we are asking for help. It is meaningful to care for and lift up other people, and to know other people care about what is happening to you and are lifting you up. More than that, the experience of communal support is a powerful anchor of well-being. But the thing is, to benefit and belong to such communities, especially inter-racial communities, I need to be vulnerable myself. No one is going to want me around merely to bear witness to what's keeping them up at night. To belong, I must be honest about my own fears and anxieties. To do that, I need to be honest with myself, be authentic, real. I do not need to collapse other people's experience into mine, or center my own experience, my own "white tears", as it were, as the most important priority of the group. But the sharing of vulnerabilities must be, in some degree, reciprocal, in order to benefit from the deep well-being that "communion" brings, the concurrent shedding of both narcissism and loneliness. I have to be vulnerable to experience, in Baldwin's terms, the sensuality of breaking bread with another that invites me to earn my life and face my death.

When I express vulnerability, I give up a certain degree of power. There is power in inhabiting the subject position where other people are objects and where I can posit myself as a virtuous voyeur. Such are *doxic* stances of white people, as previous chapters have argued. But the advantage of giving up such power is giving up loneliness and stagnation. White people are still stuck in extreme loneliness. Really, we have made being lonely a moral asset. Thus, for Baldwin, too, there is no "negro problem", there is only a white-people problem. When he exhorts white people to learn to love themselves, this includes the necessity of seeing oneself as one is and not projecting our own fears of humiliation and mortality onto black people. So, a certain degree of self-knowledge is a precursor to love.

> Therefore, a vast amount of the energy that goes into what we call the Negro problem is produced by the white man's profound desire not to be judged by those who are not white, not to be seen as he is, and at the same

time a vast amount of the white anguish is rooted in the white man's equally profound need to be seen as he is, to be released from the tyranny of his mirror. All of us know, whether or not we are able to admit it, that mirrors can only lie, that death by drowning is all that awaits one there. It is for this reason that love is so desperately sought and so cunningly avoided. Love takes off the masks that we fear we cannot live without and know we cannot live within. I use the word "love" here not merely in the personal sense but as a state of being, or a state of grace—not in the infantile American sense of being made happy but in the tough and universal sense of quest and daring and growth.

Public daring and growth sounds more alive than Arendt's version of action. That white people need to give up the "false mirror" of invulnerability to embrace mortality and act in public sounds, in some ways, like Arendt's appeal to show oneself in the polis, the space of appearances of the human being. But where Arendt's *polis* may have only existed on some imagined plane of ancient Greece, Baldwin is pushing open his *polis* in and through his writing. His writing leaves a public space in its wake, a space where a white person could arrive, invited, to kill his own innocence. Baldwin's disdain for the puerile idea of love as happiness sounds in some ways like Arendt's disdain for the social as the source of all meaning in modernity, wherein one is a slave to private interests. But, again, for Arendt, one could not love in public. What Baldwin is doing is opening a public space as the condition of the possibility for love.

NOTES

1. Nabeel Hamdi, *The Spacemaker's Guide to Big Change: Design and Improvisation in Development Practice* (London: Earthscan, 2014).
2. Patrisse Khan-Cullors describes one of the first actions of BLM, after the killing of Trayvon Martin, which she led in Beverly Hills specifically to target white, liberal audiences. Patrisse Khan-Cullors and Asha Bandele, *When They Call you a Terrorist: A Black Lives Matter Memoir* (New York: St. Martins, 2018) 200.
3. Sandra Harding has long pointed to the ways in which absolute claims of scientific objectivity are still value-driven. See her work on feminist standpoint theory in *The Science Question in Feminism* (Ithaca: Cornell UP, 1986) and also *The Feminist Standpoint Theory Reader* (New York and London: Routledge, 2004).

4. Political scientists like Bruce Bueno de Mesquita claim they can predict social movements using game theory. See *The Predictioneer's Game: Using the Logic of Brazen Self-Interest to see and Shape the Future* (New York: Random House, 2010) Even if Bueno de Mesquita is correct, there is difference between predicting that a social movement would happen given social unrest, and predicting the tactics of that social movement would influence its outcomes and cultural meaning.

5. David McIvor, *Mourning in America: Race and the Politics of Loss* (Ithaca: Cornell UP, 2016) 220.

6. *The Journal of Political Philosophy*, "Symposium on Black Lives Matter", Volume 25, issue 2, June 2017.

7. Keeanga-Yahmatta Taylor, *From #BlackLivesMatter to Black Liberation* (Chicago: Haymarket, 2016) 5.

8. Hannah Arendt, *The Human Condition*, Second Ed. (Chicago: University of Chicago Press, 1958) 177.

9. Ibid., 178.

10. James Baldwin, "Letter from a Region in My Mind", *The New Yorker*, November 17. 1962.

11. Taylor, *From #BlackLivesMatter*, 154.

12. It is not for me to give an intellectual history of BLM, as Taylor and Lebron do. Thus, I am not claiming that BLM's intellectual inheritance is solely or primarily from the Civil Rights Movement, or from the Black Power, Black Feminism, or any other historical movement. I do not have the knowledge background to make such a claim and further, I think it is for the activists themselves to describe where they are drawing their evolving intellectual heritage, which they do. See, for instance, https://blacklivesmatter.com/about/what-we-believe/. See also Opal Tometi's excellent blog, at https://www.opaltometi.org/blog/. See also Patrisse Cullors' interview with Krista Tippett, "The Spiritual Work of Black Lives Matter", at https://onbeing.org/programs/patrisse-cullors-and-robert-ross-the-spiritual-work-of-black-lives-matter-may2017/

13. See, for instance, Brian Lyman, "Selma and the Advertiser: Indifferent Coverage, Hostile Editorials", *Montgomery Advertiser*, March 1, 2015.

14. Taylor, *From #BlackLivesMatter*, 167.

15. Khan-Cullors, *When They Call You a Terrorist*.

16. Taylor, *From #BlackLivesMatter*, 168.

17. Ibid., 176.

18. See Eesha Pandit's article, "Hurricane Relief in the Spirit of Ella Baker", *In These Times*, October 11, 2017. http://inthesetimes.com/article/20578/hurricane-relief-ella-baker-harvey-blmhtx "The leaders of BLMHTX have worked in this deliberate and determined way since the organization's founding about two years ago. Their philosophy of social change is rooted

in Ella Baker's model of community organizing: decentralized, local leadership with a focus on direct action, education and community empowerment. They eschew the common tendency then (and now) to value only charismatic male leadership. BLMHTX's leaders center humility, resist centralized power, and strive to stay accountable to their community above all else."

19. The claim is not here that BLM is categorized by forgiveness. The claim is rather that BLM is unprecedented in the same way that forgiveness, for Arendt, was unprecedented.
20. Arendt, *The Human Condition*, 241.
21. Arendt writes, "In contrast to revenge, which is the natural, automatic reaction to transgression and which because of the irreversibility of the action process can be expected and even calculated, the act of forgiving can never be predicted; it is the only reaction that acts in an unexpected way and thus retains, though being a reaction, something of the original character of action. Forgiving, in other words, is the only reaction which does not merely re-act but acts anew and unexpectedly, unconditioned by the act which provoked it and therefore freeing from its consequences both the one who forgives and the one who is forgiven. The freedom contained in Jesus' teachings of forgiveness is the freedom from vengeance, which incloses both doer and sufferer in the relentless automatism of the action process, which by itself need never come to an end." *HC*, 241.
22. Martha Nussbaum, *Anger and Forgiveness: Resentment, Generosity, and Justice* (Oxford: Oxford UP, 2016).
23. My claim here is not that King was urging his audience to forgive their white transgressors, only that he was not urging vengeance.
24. Arendt, *Human Condition*, 133n.
25. Khan-Cullors, *When They Call You a Terrorist*, 200.
26. Arendt, HC, 198.
27. Khan-Cullors, 206.
28. Arendt, HC, 225.
29. Arendt, HC, 225.
30. Arendt, HC, 227.
31. Ella Baker, "Developing Community Leadership", taped interview with Gerda Lerner, December, 1970. https://poweru.org/wp-content/uploads/2015/09/baker_leadership.pdf
32. Charles Payne, "Ella Baker and Models of Social Change", *Signs*, 14.4, 1989. 893.
33. See John Stuart Mill's theory of political self-sufficiency, Mill, On Liberty, in *Three Essays* (Oxford: Oxford University Press, 1975).
34. Payne, 895.
35. Ibid., 894.

36. Ibid., 893.
37. Ibid., 11.
38. D.A. Schon, *The Reflective Practitioner: How Professionals Think in Action* (New York: Basic Books, 1983).
39. Hamdi, 80–81.
40. Ibid., 85.
41. Arendt, "Reflections on Little Rock", In *The Portable Hannah Arendt* (New York: Penguin, 2003).
42. Kathryn Gines, *Hannah Arendt and the Negro Question* (Bloomington: Indiana UP, 2014) 6.
43. Juliet Hooker writes that: "the photograph upon which Arendt based her critique of black parents and the NAACP did not in fact depict a young black girl forced to face a racist white mob alone. Instead, Dorothy Counts was accompanied both by a black friend of the family (who Arendt assumed was white, despite the fact that he was identified as black in the accompanying article) and by her father." "Black Lives Matter and the Paradoxes of U.S. Black Politics: From Democratic Sacrifice to Democratic Repair", *Political Theory*, April 4, 2016. 459. documents.
44. For this insight and its full consequences, I thank the anonymous reviewers at Palgrave Macmillan.
45. Hannah Arendt, *Essays in Understanding, 1930–1954: Formation, Exile, and Totalitarianism* (New York: Schocken, 2005) 12.
46. Gines, 2.
47. See for instance, Seyla Benhabib, *The Reluctant Modernism of Hannah Arendt* (New York: Rowman and Littlefield, 2003). Also, Michael D. Burroughs, "Hannah Arendt, 'Reflections on Little Rock,' and White Ignorance" *Critical Philosophy of Race*, Vol. 3, No. 1 (2015), pp. 52–78. Also Christopher Phillip Long, "A Fissure in the Distinction: Hannah Arendt, the Family, and the Public Realm", Philosophy and Social Criticism, Sept. 1, 998.
48. Gines, 58. Gines writes, "Arendt's attempts to parse segregation within her theoretical grid does not work. The political, private, and social realms are not as clear-cut as her paradigm suggests. Social and political inequalities are interconnected and reinforce one another." 47.
49. Arendt, *The Life of the Mind: The Groundbreaking Investigation on How We Think* (New York: Harcourt, 1978) 158.
50. Gines, 19.
51. Arendt: "I should like to remind the reader that I am writing as an outsider. I have never lived in the South and have even avoided occasional trips to Southern states because they would have brought me into a situation that I personally found unbearable. Like most people of European origin I have difficulty in understanding, let alone sharing, the common prejudices

of Americans in this area … I should like to make it clear that as a Jew I take my sympathy for the cause of the Negroes as for all the oppressed or under-privileged peoples for granted and should appreciate it if the reader did likewise." "Reflections on Little Rock," 46.

52. Balwdin's essay "A Letter from a Region in my Mind" would later become the larger part of *The Fire Next Time.*

53. Baldwin, *The Fire Next Time* (New York: Random House, 1993) 9.

54. Ibid., 92.

55. Ibid., 43.

56. Augustine. *The Confessions of St. Augustine.* Thomas A. Kempis, trans. (New York: Collier, 1909) 52.

57. Baldwin, 30.

58. Ibid., 58.

59. Ibid., 30.

CHAPTER 5

Conclusion

5.1 Interrogating Allyship

In this final chapter, I want to return to interrogating the self-described "ally" of black-led social movements, which is really an interrogation of my own identity as a white feminist. I feel ill at ease with the white self-description of allyship involving only belief (I believe black lives deserve dignity) and not even the kind of risk and action that Baldwin demands (commitment, presence, and vulnerability). Also, I address one final intellectual objection to BLM, a concern about identity politics, and read the objection as one more dodge away from commitment and solidarity. I reiterate what this book's primary goal has been, that is, to challenge some of the impediments a white audience might have in respecting BLM. I do not give any positive theory of an ally or resolve the problems of allyship in any absolute manner—I am not sure such a theory is possible—but I do give some positive possible landscapes for empathy.

5.2 Answering Objections to Identity Politics

There is a last and looming objection to BLM which need to be addressed, as it is serious and thoughtful. Political theorists and the white public alike articulate concerns about identity politics in general. Mark Lilla is an exemplar of this view, and he is not alone.[1] Lilla believes that liberals in the United States have moved toward valuing identity politics at their own peril. Lilla defines identity politics as partitioning of different identity

© The Author(s) 2019
J. C. Luttrell, *White People and Black Lives Matter*,
https://doi.org/10.1007/978-3-030-22489-9_5

categories over and against unifying on the basis of common citizenship, and he argues it represents a death knell for effective political power. If liberal political theorists of Lilla's ilk dismiss BLM, they tend to do so because they are skeptical of the broader vision of identity politics' capacity to achieve a fair society.[2] Their skepticism is not in all ways unwarranted. In *New and Old Wars: Organized Violence in a Global Era*, Mary Kaldor points to backward-looking identity politics as a causal factor in violent conflict. However, there is a difference between the kind of ethnic nationalism that is prone to conflict and inimical to justice, and the hopeful, forward-looking, creation and affirmation of communities. Here, I outline the differences between the types of identity politics that create conflict and identity politics that uncover already-occurring conflict in order to resolve it. BLM belongs firmly in the latter category.

Lilla gives the most vehement and current critique of identity politics. It is a critique I suspect a broader white public shares, in various degrees and *doxas*, and so it is worth addressing. My response to Lilla reviews of this book's central theme: the imperfection and possibility of empathy across different identities. His book *The Once and Future Liberal* is a tome about how the Democratic Party has lost its way by kowtowing to social movements like Black Lives Matter. For Lilla, movements of identity are anti-political; they are over-individualistic, and instead of encouraging young people to work together on behalf of a common good, they throw people back on themselves, encouraging myopia and self-obsession of a social-media-obsessed generation. His position is that modern forms of identity politics undermine themselves. By emphasizing difference, they further disenfranchise minorities and oppressed peoples, the very populations they are out to empower. Marked by a "resentful, disuniting rhetoric of difference", it becomes impossible to form a common language to persuade people of different backgrounds to unite in a common cause.[3] The impossibility of common dialogue becomes exceedingly evident when academics (like myself) want to claim that different groups have different epistemologies, some more privileged than others regarding their own experience. Lilla asks, "if you believe identity determines everything. It means that there is no impartial space for dialogue. White men have one 'epistemology', black women have another. So what remains to be said?"[4] If, Lilla contends, different groups share different knowledges, therefore no common ground for discussion can possible be found, and argument itself is annihilated replaced only by taboo. Lilla continues, "only those with an approved identity status are, like shamans, allowed to speak on certain matters. Particular groups—today the trans-gendered—are given temporary totemic significance."[5] The loss of a common ground of identification, which is for Lilla the loss of a sense of citizenship and shared public duty, is lamentable precisely because, when oppressed groups need to advocate for their rights, they are further alienated from common political spaces. The democratic party, he contends, has lost any shared language. What a shared language for Lilla would mean would be "reaching out to the working class" and paying attention to the land between the coasts.[6] Instead, he excoriates liberals for "[becoming] enthralled with social movements" operating outside foundational government institutions.[7]

Of BLM, Lilla writes,

> black lives matter is a textbook example of how not to build solidarity ... there is no denying that by publicizing and protesting police mistreatment of African-Americans the movement mobilized supporters and delivered a wake-up call to every American with a conscience. But there is also no denying that the movement's decision to use this mistreatment to build a general indictment of American society, and its law enforcement institutions, and to use Mau-Mau tactics to put down dissent and demand a confession of sins and public penitence (most spectacularly in a public confrontation with Hillary Clinton, of all people), played into the hands of the Republican right.[8]

In other words, even though Lilla believes BLM's cause to be just, he disdains its tactics. This, as I have said, is the most common liberal response, and I have given a sustained criticism of it in Chap. 4. I read the critique of BLM's form as an excuse not to engage with its content, and I argued activists themselves are in the best position to know whether a strategy will be successful, and how to best define success. Lilla also compares BLM to the Civil Rights Movement, and in doing so, he sterilizes the civil rights' revolutionary aims. As I have discussed in Chaps. 2 and 4, that comparison between civil rights and BLM is a white *doxa*, a common habit and assumed truth. He incorrectly implies that the Civil Rights movement did not give an indictment to broader American society, which, as I discuss at length in Chap. 1, is a common and gross misreading of even the singularity of King's "I have a Dream Speech", let alone the broader movement, including SNCC and the Southern Christian Leadership Conference. To review briefly, King assured his audience that "The whirlwind of revolt will continue to shake the foundation of America until the bright days of justice emerge" and emphasizes that "We can never be satisfied as long as the Negro is the victim of the unspeakable horrors of police brutality."[9] To say that even King's message did not include a general indictment of the American public is a common "white-washing" by liberals of the Civil Rights Movement to make it fit the liberal goals and aims, which do not include a thoroughgoing revision of the basic institutions of society. The call to "shake the foundations" of American society is a call to make just America's basically unjust institutions. Here, though Lilla's comparison between BLM and the Civil Rights Movement is worthy of further analysis, I am only noting that the comparison forms the substructure of his critique of identity politics, an appraisal that is, as I have said, one that I suspect is widely shared amongst the white, liberal public.

Again, for Lilla, the Civil Rights Movement was fundamentally different from Black Lives Matter because it did not "build a general indictment of American society and its law enforcement institutions". Such an indictment, Lilla argues, alienates the majority of white citizens from joining the cause, and is self-defeating, undermining, as does most identity politics, a shared sense of "we". Rather, he argues, the Civil Rights movement was constructive; it inspired America to live up to its universal principles. "The leaders of the civil rights movement chose to take the concept of universal, equal citizenship more seriously than white America ever had. Not to idealize or deny difference—which was evident to the naked eye—but to render it politically impotent."[10] It allowed white America to identify with black America on the basis of universal citizenship. Lilla contends that BLM fails to accomplish the same ends, because it resists identification across race.

> "Given the segregation in American society white families have little chance of seeing and therefore understanding the lives of black Americans. I am not a black male motorist and never will be. All the more reason, then, that I need some way to identify with him if I am going to be affected by his experience. And citizenship is the only thing we share. The more the differences between us are emphasized, the less likely I will be to feel outrage at his treatment."[11]

In Lilla's statement, I find one of the central and motivating questions of my inquiry: *Can* white people understand? And, *will* they? Returning to Chap. 1, I find such are questions of ability, motivation, and willing. Lilla confuses motivation for ability. Lilla quickly assumes he cannot empathize with different experience unless he shares a common identification. This is the very problem, as I discuss in Chap. 2, with which Adam Smith wrestles. For Smith, and for myself, empathizing across differences sans common identification is the mark of adulthood and civilization. Such empathy is neither a foregone conclusion nor even a very predictable outcome of any given encounter, but it is possible. The point is that one must practice and try, that is, give attention, "the time of day", and "tarry" in the first place. I do not need a common identification of "citizen" to imperfectly but meaningfully hold space open for my friend's grief at having lost their child. Indeed, in a global society, to say I am friends only with those whom I share citizenship would be very strange. Furthermore, white supremacy excludes black people from the markers of citizenship before the fact, so common identification can never get off the ground. Thus, we must empathize without common identity.[12] Even though I did not experience what others experienced, and probably never will, I can act in ways that let them feel less alone in their grief, and I can honor their mourning. Empathy builds friendship, and friendship encourages empathy; one is not, under the Smithean account, a precursor to another. The process is dialectical. Lilla assumes that America's segregation is a stable fact rather than a contingent, dynamic process. If BLM's work is in part to counter the segregation of experience precisely by mourning in white, public spaces, what is self-defeating is not BLM's tactics but white responses themselves which maintain they cannot empathize across difference in the first place.

That some people know more about their own experience, that they have different epistemologies, does not mean, ipso facto, that we have no common ground of discussion. It does mean that it is probably best to start discussing the difference of experience by one person talking and the other person listening. If I care about the person, I might avoid entering into dialogue with them first demanding that they show me what goals and aims we both share. Instead, I might come to share their goals in the process of empathizing. It is on me to reign in my own self-defeating tactics of dialogue which undermine the possibility of discussion from the outset. If I am motivated to stop and give the content of what's being said "the time of day", learning is possible. My own learning does not need to be perfect in order for me to work in solidarity to accomplish some political goals. That is, I do not need to perfectly or absolutely inhabit the other's perspective, demanding no remainder, in order to engage with them. Such a demand is impossible, but I might cling to it if I did not want to give my interlocutor my full attention. This act of listening and learning is, for Smith and myself, the very vehicle of *ecstasis*,[13] of getting out of oneself, and escaping the solipsism and self-obsession that Lilla worries characterizes so much of modern political life.

Lilla lauds the Civil Rights Movement for emphasizing an ideal of institutional colorblindness. "The movement", he writes, "shamed America into action by consciously appealing to what we share, so that it became harder for white Americans to keep two sets of books, psychologically speaking: one for 'Americans' and one for 'Negroes'.[14] This description of public shaming might be correct, but BLM is working in a different era, one where the post-civil rights promises of institutional and legalistic colorblindness have failed to protect the rights and lives of Black Americans. Given the steady undermining of civil rights era gains in the 1980s and 1990s, BLM activists have wised up."[15] Taylor writes, "if a central demand of the civil rights movement in the 1960s was federal intervention to act against discrimination and act affirmatively to improve the quality of life for African Americans, promoting the United States as colorblind or post-racial has done the opposite as it is used to justify dismantling the state's capacity to challenge discrimination."[16] In other words, colorblindness has been tried, and it failed to curb police brutality, the school-to-prison pipeline, mass incarceration, unequal segregation, and any number of other social ills to which BLM points, including the murder of black citizens. Lilla's demand that BLM use the idealized and colorblind language of citizenship to promote its goals—or else he is less likely to listen to them—comes in a time precisely when legalistic and institutional colorblindness has failed to keep black people from being murdered, much less from achieving any semblance of formal equality. So, there are indeed important ways in which BLM is *not like* the Civil Rights movement, especially the white mis-remembrance of Civil Rights, but it is precisely those ways which it is important for white people to respect.

As I discussed in Chap. 2, Charles Mills writes extensively on this issue of the failure of colorblindness and post-racialism.[17] Mills contends, and I agree, that forms of racism are fluid. Racist practices used to be justified more explicitly, on the pseudo-scientific basis that blackness constituted a lesser form of humanity. Now debunked, racist practices continue precisely because we live in a society that insists it is *already* post-racial, that is, colorblind. Under this view, the Civil Rights Movement was successful in garnering equal rights and protection for black populations in the

United States. If racial justice has already been achieved, it is impossible to see the non-ideal realities of injustice. In this context, colorblind aspirations take on an obscuring function. To be clear, Lilla does not hold this view that the United States has already achieved racial justice, but it is precisely this notion of "post-racialism" which BLM is destabilizing. It would be self-defeating to destabilize assumptions of colorblindness by appealing to colorblindness itself. Yet, that is what Lilla and many white liberals demand.

Finally, Lilla advises against the political use of identity politics because, if not nativism itself, it invites nativism into the room. "As soon as you cast an issue exclusively in terms of identity you invite your adversary to do the same. Those who play one race card should be prepared to be trumped by another, as we saw subtly and not so subtly in the 2016 presidential election."[18] I assume he means, in part, that BLM activists invited the blatant displays of white supremacists beliefs into the mainstream of American politics, in ways white liberals thought were not possible at this time in history. Yet, it is reductive to lump all identity politics into one category, and it assumes a uniform lack of intelligence, an inability to differentiate different political projects, on the part of these movements' audiences. Lilla's worry echoes the worry I addressed in Chap. 1, that if I speak of race at all, if I name whiteness, it is a slippery slope to white supremacy. (I do not want to replicate the white supremacists' insistence that race has an ontological status.) But, of course, one could believe that race has social significance without essentializing it. In addition, there is more than one kind of identity politics.

Good work on identity politics is being done in studies on the changing character of war. The worries which come from this field about identity politics contributing to violent conflict are instructive. Mary Kaldor expresses the most cogent version of the concern. First, she defines her terms: "I use the term 'identity politics' to mean movements which mobilize around ethnic, racial, or religious identity for the purpose of claiming state power."[19] Kaldor distinguishes two kinds of identity politics: backward-looking and forward-looking. Backward-looking identity politics are both a symptom and contributing factor to modern forms of violent conflict. Backward-looking identity politics tends to be nostalgic, imagining some romantic past and false homogeneity.[20] In contrast, forward-looking identity politics are not a causal factor in modern conflicts. In fact, they tend to be the opposite; they are promoters of peace and modern cosmopolitanism. Backward-looking politics are exclusivist, often characterized by "the victim mentality often characteristic of majorities who feel themselves minorities", and media campaigns which do not value factual evidence.[21] Backward-looking identity politics acquire power through a sense of being threatened by different labels. In contrast, forward-looking identity politics are integrative, embracing all participants who support the common political vision. In general, they do not attempt to purge one segment of society from a political voice; they aim to include more. Forward-looking identity politics can be based on ideas, like freedom and dignity. For instance, Kaldor writes, "The politics of ideas is about forward-looking projects. ... [such as] Early nationalist struggles ... in colonial Africa were about democracy and state building. They were conceived as ways of welding together diverse groups of people under the rubric of nation for the purpose of modernization."[22] Crucially, Kaldor writes that political campaigns to promote religion or culture that lead to demands for power in order to ensure that policies are adopted are *not* the corrosive, backward-looking kinds of identity politics which contribute to conflict. Rather, "the demand for political rights on the basis of identity as opposed to the demand for power on the basis of a political program" are the kinds of backward-looking politics which typically contribute to conflict.[23]

Black Lives Matter is a forward-looking identity politics. It is inclusive. As I have outlined, it is a collaboration between many different coalitions, which have many different concrete goals but basically one single driving idea: the freedom and dignity of black people and the sanctity and respect for black lives. That is an *idea*, not an identity. White people can also work in solidarity for the freedom and dignity of black people, and they are invited to do so. BLM is not demanding political power for black people, because they are black. It is working for political power so that black people are protected from terror. In terms of political representation, there is a higher probability—though not certainty—that people of color will understand and be committed to the urgency and profundity of that demand, given they are closer to the experience. Further, black leaders are centered in the rich cultural context which already values black lives, a culture which gives them a wellspring and cornerstone for their work. For this reason and others, BLM invites everyone to participate, but not for everyone to lead. That is a fair invitation. In contrast, social movements for white supremacy are not advocating for merely an idea, the dignity and freedom of white people; they are advocating for white power on the basis of exclusivist identities. Reasonable people can see that there is no moral or political equivalence here.

From close up, it is apparent that the intersectional activism which BLM promotes and employs is precisely the kind of thing Kaldor describes about positive identity politics that gather together diverse coalitions for a broad, visionary, future-oriented politics.[24] For instance, the BLM:HTX (Black Lives Matter: Houston, Texas) chapter has long promoted intersectional, "Black and Brown" coalitions, and it works closely with groups like United We Dream on immigration issues which affect the Latino community. Intersectionality precisely means that one refuses to be constrained into a narrow set—a singular line—of identity-based interests.[25] Regarding black-brown alliances in Houston, Frances Valdez, a community activist on behalf of the group United We Dream, explains, "Many of us hold multiple identities ourselves, like black, brown, queer, trans, undocumented and so many others, so you're not going to be able to hold on to the idea that immigrants only care about immigrant issues, and queer people only care about LGBT rights and so on."[26]

Furthermore, the assumption that BLM is exclusionary relies on somewhat essentialist identity category of blackness. As Tommy Shelby contends, there is no essentialist black identity one can point to within movements fighting anti-black racism, nor need there be. Shelby describes his aim to "disentangle ... the call for black political solidarity from collective black identity."[27] There are plural modes of blackness, and any claimed essentialist mode is contested. That modes of identity are plural and contested, though, need not be a barrier to political action. BLM does not promote looking inside oneself eternally to figure out one's true "identity" in order to be involved. Again, one not need share an identity category to work in political solidarity. So, even if there is disagreement amongst BLM chapters about how intersectional they want to be, and worries about mission-drift, even "solely" black movements themselves are coalitions of different identities.

A movement like BLM which *uncovers* existing injustice so as not to inflict future injustice is not a conflict-producing identity politics. As a campaign that works against white supremacy, it in fact undermines America's most pernicious version of backward-looking identity politics. BLM is a forward-looking project, one that promotes peace. BLM's credentials as a peace movement were recently recognized, when the three founders were awarded the Sydney Peace Prize for Activism.[28] The white liberal insistence that BLM is a conflict-producing, backward-looking, and essentializing identity politics, even when presented with evidence to the contrary in the form of intersectional coalitions and statements of idea-driven visions, points to a recalcitrance, narcissism, immobility, or unwillingness on the part of white liberals, not a failing of BLM.

5.3   WHITE FEMINISM AND ALLYSHIP

The white liberal critique that advises "be inclusive or I will not listen" reminds me, again, of Mrs. Williard's self-description as a "well-wisher" to Ida B. Wells-Barnett's Reconstruction-era anti-lynching campaign, out paradigmatic "ally". Mrs. Williard's "well-wishing" on behalf of Northern Women's Temperance leagues functioned less as political solidarity and more as veiled warning.[29] Again, Mrs. Williard essentially advised Wells-Barnett that she was only on her side in so far as she did not impugn her colleagues—white women—in the South. If she did, Wells would alienate white people, her mission would be self-defeating, and she could no longer support the cause. Mrs. Williard critiqued the form of the message while purporting to support its content. In Wells' words, "Miss Willard protests against lynching in one paragraph and then, in the next, deliberately misrepresents my position in order that she may criticise a movement, whose only purpose is to protect our oppressed race from vindictive slander and Lynch Law."[30] Wells rightly points out that Mrs. Williard did not, in fact, support the content of the anti-lynching campaign. Wells' message was to tell the truth, and the truth was that southern white women were lying about their relationships with black men. White women's lies were part of the vehicle of lynching, and in order to destabilize the cultural support for lynching, Wells needed to honestly analyze each cultural phenomenon which gave it support. Given her positionality as a writer from the black press in Memphis, she was in a better position than the Northern Women's Temperance Leagues to know what the most effective anti-lynching campaign tactic would be.

Mrs. Williard's comments are predictive of the history of white feminism responding to black-led movements for social justice.[31] White feminism is not really that distinct from white liberalism. The history of white feminism offers an example of a notorious failure of empathy. I find bell hooks' critique of white feminism to be the clearest. hooks described her experience being part of early feminist consciousness raising groups, in the 1970s and 1980s, when she tried to share her own, different experiences from the white feminists in the group.[32] The white women became defensive and told hooks her experiences and goals were inimical to feminism as a whole. hooks spend a while wondering if she was, indeed, a feminist, and if feminism had a place for her. hooks' disillusionment is indicative of a larger trend in white feminism.[33]

Mariana Ortega's article, "Being Lovingly, Knowingly Ignorant: White Feminist and Women of Color" opens up the problems of self-described allyship.[34] Ortega notes that white feminists often inhabit a particular space where they are aware of historical oppressive and inaccurate descriptions of women of color and want to do better. They do not want to collapse all difference and create a homogenous space of agreement. Further, they want to be "loving", to see and treat women of color respectfully. Yet, standing at the intersection of knowledge and desired virtue, white feminism still holds on to ignorance. Ortega writes "Thus we may find the feminist who wants to perceive lovingly, who wants to see women of color in their own terms, does not want to homogenize them, does not want to be coercive with them, does not want to use them but who, despite her well intentions, turns women of color into something that can be used to further her own desires."[35] Ortega gives examples of white feminists who collapse all "women of color" into one category or tokenize insights from scholars to reinforce their own work. As a white woman, I may think I am giving recognition to women of color, but I still, too often, prioritize myself. As Baldwin perceives, I am mostly prioritizing my own desire to be loved and accepted, or at least to be forgiven. I cannot yet give love, acceptance, and forgiveness to myself because I do not yet realize that I need these things. I have not yet faced the dark spots within myself to be self-aware enough to realize what I am asking.

Many white feminists who support BLM engage in the discourse of allyship. In different ways, we ask for love and acceptance from black activists, and in doing so rank our own needs—unknown to ourselves—over the movement. To say that one is an ally is essentially to state that one empathizes with the experiences being expressed in the movement. However, allyship becomes its own identity marker, and one given to quietism. Allyship itself is subject to Lilla's critique of identity politics—it becomes a myopic and static self-description, rather than a way to describe motivation for political engagement. Often in allyship, white women's own experience remains centered; it is our own identity as an "ally" that becomes important, rather than the experiences of those in the movement. Allies can be given to excessive statements about themselves, often on social media, rather than sustained collaborative action with social movements. These allies fail to achieve what Adam Smith thought empathy was doing: getting oneself out of one's own ego and stepping outside of the particularly harmful stance of impartiality that takes one's own experiences as the paradigm for all possible stories. That kind of empathy, again, can only be achieved in genuine, face-to-face interaction and honest self-reflection.

Again, honest self-reflection is not easy. Writer Joan Didion agrees. She writes, "self-deception remains the most difficult deception."[36] Didion's essay, "On Self-Respect" is fabulous in that it could be a road map for would-be allies. Didion describes a time as a young woman when she failed entry into an honor society, an accolade she expected she should have, and was, for the first time faced with contingency rather than a certainty of her privilege. "I lost the conviction that lights would always turn green for me … lost a certain touching faith in the totem power of good manners, clean hair, and proven competence on the Stanford-Binet scale. To such doubtful amulets had my self-respect been pinned". Her portrayal of herself is outstanding because it describes, in near perfection I think, the growing pains of realizing that I do not get what I want merely based on good intentions. Needing to find a more secure footing for self-regard, real self-respect, she writes, has more to do with taking responsibility for one's own life than good intentions and good-girl charm. It is being able to sleep at night not despite, but along with, an accurate accounting of the less-than-wonderful things one has done. People with self-respect "know the price of things." They do not, for example, go running for absolution from their partners after an affair. The crucial thing for Didion, though, is that self-respect means that one is indeed sleeping, and soundly. One is not mired in an evangelical amount of guilt, watching a home movie of all the horrible things one has done and the moral mistakes made. The reason those with self-respect can sleep at night is precisely that they are humble and authentic enough to make friends and be a friend. They are free to be humble because they are not chained to inhabiting a false virtue in front of an adoring audience. Didion writes, "To have that sense of one's intrinsic worth which, for better or for worse, constitutes self-respect, is potentially to have everything: the ability to discriminate, to love and to remain indifferent. To lack it is to be locked within oneself, paradoxically incapable of either love or indifference."

Sometimes the discourse of allyship and white privilege can be stuck in the sort of evangelical framework, a paradigm wherein racism is a "sin", and where it is the state of the white person's soul that's important.[37] The white person can "confess" their privilege, and once this is done, I hope to be "absolved" of racism. People of color in this exchange become vessels of redemption, rather than complex agents in their own right. This paradigm of sin also gives rise to defensiveness ("white talk"), where white people who have, like everyone, faced hardship and suffering in our lives, and chafe at the idea that we have privilege on the basis of being white because they take white privilege to mean committing some sort of sinful transgression.[38] We claim innocence.[39] While conversations about the state of the soul of white America are surely useful, especially in churches and religious contexts, discussions of allyship that continue to conclude on the topic of white innocence, absolution, or guilt miss the point. They are not empathetic, because empathy comes after self-respect.

5.4   A Positive Prescription for Empathy?

Besides understanding BLM in the lens of political action, much of this book's argument has been critical. I have pointed out problematic white responses to BLM and inserted skepticism into those responses. Yet, critique can only go so far. What, then, if any, is a positive white response to BLM? Beyond critique, are there normative prescriptions to be made?

In one sense, I am not convinced it is very useful for a philosopher to explain how empathy works, primarily because it would be redundant. In our own families and friends' groups, we already know how to empathize. It does not require a Ph.D. To the contrary, graduate school taught me that academics are often the worst people to advise in matters of emotional intelligence. Functioning adults (if not academics) already take time to be with others, to listen, and allow the people we care about the full range of human emotion, complexity, contradictions, ambiguity, and support that we would want to give ourselves. It is just that, for the most part, we reserve those kindnesses for other white people, those whom we know well, and we do not, overall, empathize across difference.

The contact hypothesis speaks to the ways in which empathy is, if not predictable, at least possible, if a person spends a significant amount of time with differently raced others. However, given the realities of entrenched segregation in the United States, it is tempting to abandon empathy all together, as Bloom advocates. Or, instead, resign oneself to segregation but find unifying identity categories like "citizen" across segregated spaces, as Lilla proposes. Another option, however, is fighting segregation in the first place. That is exactly what BLM is doing. In Taylor's accounting, BLM ruptures the segregation of experiences. The movement gives rich expressions and profound voice to previously silenced experiences, in public spaces like restaurants, shopping malls, and street intersections. It does not take a lifetime of close friendship with black people to listen and believe the narratives and perspectives BLM expresses. One can also hear these messages in Kendrick Lamar or Beyoncé songs, on the radio, on the way to work. It is a sad irony that, at the exact moment BLM attempts to counter the segregation of institutional experiences, the white liberal response is lament the fact of segregation in the first place, rather than to engage with the content of what is being said.

So, how should one engage? The very act of stopping what one is doing, putting on hold one's own aims and objectives to take time and listen to another person are the beginning of engagement. Busyness is a status symbol in American culture, and it is necessary to put those aspirations to status aside for a moment, in engaging with moral social movements outside of one's own private interest.[40] In the vein of "taking the time of day", George Yancy uses the language of "tarrying".[41] In tarrying, I hear echoes of staying a little longer, not leaving the scene, not bailing out. There is also an open-endedness to tarrying, both in terms of goals and time. Because tarrying is meant to encourage an encounter, there is not a pre-ordained outcome to such an encounter—the outcome is created in the relationship itself.

Here I am encouraging a need for white people to "tarry" with black-led social movements, to allow for open-ended encounters, to bracket their own objectives for a moment and dwell, imperfectly, in the narrative of another's experience. Because BLM, as did Civil Rights, involves an indictment of white America, "tarrying" involves staying with the uncomfortability of self-reflection. George Yancy encourages white people to tarry in with the uncomfortability of their own whiteness. Yancy writes, and I quote at length:

> The call to tarry is indeed a *clarion* call, loud and direct: it is designed to encourage white people not to move too quickly when confronted with the muck and mire of their own whiteness. Rather, it is about how much of one's opaque white racist self, and one's social embedded reality in the structures of white supremacy, can be uncovered, identified, faced, and challenged. The trick is not to flee, but to have the foundations of one's white being challenged, to lose one's sense of white self-certainty and to render unstable that familiar white sense of being-in-the-world. The process of tarrying encourages forms of courageous listening, humility, and the capacity to be touched, to be shaken by those black bodies and bodies of color that have achieved and honed degrees of epistemic complexity regarding white racism, forms of knowing that result from being raced targets of a system that privileges white bodies and polices black bodies and bodies of color in ways that render them 'suspect', 'criminal', 'inferior'.[42]

When Yancy encourages that white people cultivate the "capacity to be touched", he emphasizes that white people must let go of a sense of mastery. To be touched, in one's body and heart, might be more of a process of *letting go*. The goal here is not to "get woke", as it were, i.e., to become proficient and master a vocabulary of social justice. Rather, the goal, if there is any, is to be *less* in control, be more vulnerable, allow oneself into an arena—another's very different experience—in which the ground of one's own knowledge is most unsteady.

Therapists have long known that empathy mostly involves non-interrupted listening, affirming the existence of other's feelings, and allowing both you and your interlocutor the full range of human emotions, including uncomfortable, inconvenient, or so-called "inappropriate" feelings.[43] In order to listen, one must first recognize structural obstacles that prevent the process of listening, such as the tendency to revert to one's own paradigmatic experience and implicit bias. Evidence-based psychotherapy advises that listeners should never assume they are mind readers, or that their experience of understanding will match their interlocutor's feeling of being understood. "Empathy should always be offered with humility and held lightly, ready to be corrected."[44] Further, there is no evidence that empathy exists without first caring for the other person.[45] One needs to first care about the well-being of another in order to empathize with them.

So, the question that began this inquiry—if white people can understand, will they?—remains. It is not settled. Likely, the question cannot be answered in philosophical argumentation. Whether people will care in the first place is a matter of action, not contemplation, to be witnessed in relationships. What I hope this work has done, in interrogating white responses to Black Lives Matter, is make room for the question to be asked a little more honestly.

NOTES

1. The objection to identity politics is widely shared. Beyond Lilla, both Sheri Berman and Jonathan Haidt hold similar positions. For instance, see Sheri Berman, "Why Identity Politics Benefits the Right more than the Left", *The Guardian*, July 14, 2018. https://www.theguardian.com/comment-isfree/2018/jul/14/identity-politics-right-left-trump-racism. See also Jonathan Haidt, "Why Nationalism Beats Globalism", *The American Interest*, Vol. 12, No.1, July 10, 2016. https://www.the-american-interest.com/2016/07/10/when-and-why-nationalism-beats-globalism/

2. I must here distinguish different types of liberalism. By "liberal", Lilla means the politics on the left in the United States, and the democratic party. My earlier discussion of liberalism in the context of Martha Nussbaum referred to liberalism in the philosophical sense, as ideal political theorists of basic institutions, resting on the twin priorities of fairness and equality, in the vein of John Rawls. Both types of liberals have miscast BLM, but in different ways.

3. Mark Lilla, *The Once and Future Liberal: After Identity Politics* (New York: Harper Collins, 2017) 59.

4. Ibid., 90.

5. Ibid., 91.

6. Lilla, 59.

7. Lilla, 59.

8. Ibid., 129.

9. Martin Luther King, Jr. "I Have a Dream...", 1963 March on Washington. https://www.archives.gov/files/press/exhibits/dream-speech.pdf

10. Lilla, 65.

11. Ibid., 128.

12. Feminist theorists like Audre Lorde and María Lugones have been emphasizing the need and possibility to empathize across difference for decades. See Audre Lorde, *Sister Outsider*, Freedom California: Crossing Press. 1984. See also María Lugones, *Pilgrimages/peregrinajes: Theorizing Coalition Against Multiple Oppressions* (Lanham, MD: Rowman and Littlefield, 2003).

13. I use the word *ecstasis* here not in the esoteric, Heidegerrian sense, but in a more every-day sense: merely an escape from narcissism, getting outside of oneself.

14. Ibid., 130.

15. Both Naomi Zack and Carol Anderson give extensive account of how the legal undermining of civil rights era legislation occurred. See Zack, *White Privilege and Black Rights: The Injustice of US Police Racial Profiling and Homicide* (NY: Rowman and Littlefield, 2015) Carol Anderson, *White Rage: The Unspoken Truth of our Racial Divide* (London and New York: Bloomsbury, 2016).

16. Keeanga-Yahmatta Taylor, *From #BlackLivesMatter to Black Liberation* (Chicago: Haymarket, 2016), 5.

17. Mills, Charles. "White Ignorance", in *Race and Epistemologies of Ignorance*, eds. Shannon Sullivan, Nancy Tuana (Albany: SUNY Press, 2007) 11–38. Also, *Black Rights, White Wrongs: The Critique of Racial Liberalism* (Oxford: Oxford UP, 2007).

18. Lilla, 129.

19. Mary Kaldor, *New and Old Wars: Organized Violence in a Global Era*. 3rd Ed. (Stanford: Stanford UP, 2006) 79.

20. Ibid., 80.

21. Ibid., 41.

22. Ibid., 80.

23. Ibid.

24. See Sharon Doetsch-Kidder, *Social Change and Intersectional Activism: The Spirit of Social Movement* (New York: Palgrave Macmillan, 2012).

25. Kimberle Crenshaw, "Mapping the Margins: Intersectionality, Identity Politics, and Violence Against Women of Color", *Stanford Law Review*, Vol. 43, 1993.

26. Eesha Pandit, "New Black–Brown Alliances in Houston could set a Pattern for Grassroots Progressive Change", *Salon*, November 7, 2016. https://www.salon.com/2016/11/07/new-black-brown-alliances-in-houston-could-set-a-pattern-for-grassroots-progressive-change/

27. Tommie Shelby, *We Who Are Dark: The Philosophical Foundations of Black Solidarity* (Cambridge: Harvard UP, 2007) 206.

28. The Sydney Peace Prize for Activism, http://sydneypeacefoundation.org.au/peace-prize-recipients/black-lives-matter/

29. Ida B. Wells-Barnett, "A Red Record" in *On Lynching* (Mineola: Dover, 2014), 29–116.

30. Ibid.

31. Feminist philosophers have written at length on white feminism's exclusions. See, for instance, Mariana Ortega, "On Being Lovingly, Knowingly Ignorant: White Feminism and Women of Color", *Hypatia*, Vol. 26, No. 3, 2006. 56–75. Naomi Zack, *Inclusive Feminism: A Third Wave Theory of Women's Commonality* (New York: Rowman and Littlefield, 2005) Patricia Hill Collins, *Black Feminist Thought* (New York: Routledge) 1991. bell hooks, *Feminist Theory: From Margin to Center* (South End Press, 1984). Sarita Srivastava, "You're calling me a racist? The Moral and Emotional Regulation of Antiracism and Feminism," *Signs the Journal of Women in Culture and Society*, 2005, Vol. 31, no. 1 (30, 44, 42–43).

32. bell hooks, "Theory as Liberatory Practice", in *Teaching to Transgress: Education as the Practice of Freedom* (NY: Routledge, 1994).

33. Kimberle Crenshaw, "Mapping the Margins: Intersectionality, Identity Politics, and Violence Against Women of Color", *Stanford Law Review*, Vol. 43, 1993.

34. Mariana Ortega, "On Being Lovingly, Knowingly Ignorant: White Feminism and Women of Color", *Hypatia*, Vol. 21, No. 3, 2006.

35. Ibid., 61.

36. Joan Didion, "On Self Respect", *Vogue*, 1961.

37. Naomi Zack, in *White Privilege and Black Rights*, notices this pattern.

38. Allison Baily, "White Talk as a Barrier to Understanding Whiteness", in George Yancy (ed.), *White Self-Criticality beyond Anti-racism: How Does It Feel to Be a White Problem?* (Lanham: Lexington, 2014) 37–57.

39. George Yancy writes, "[Tarrying] is *not* about seeing how much guilt one can endure. This sounds like a species of white self-indulgence through a mode of masochism". "Tarrying Together", *Educational Philosophy and Theory*. Vol. 27, No.1, 26–35. 26.

40. Silvia Bellezza, Neeru Paharia, and Anat Keinan. "Lack of Leisure: Busyness as the New Status Symbol", *Journal of Consumer Research*, March 22, 2017.

41. Yancy, "Tarrying Together", 26.

42. Ibid.

43. Elliot Robert, Arthur C. Bohart, Jeanne Watson, and Leslie Greenberg, "Empathy", *Psychotherapy*, Vol. 48(1), Mar, 2011. Special Issue: Evidence-Based Psychotherapy Relationships. pp. 43–49.

44. Ibid., 48.

45. Ibid., "Finally, because research has shown empathy to be inseparable from the other relational conditions, therapists should seek to offer empathy in the context of positive regard and genuineness. Empathy will not be effective unless if it is grounded in authentic caring for the client." 49.

Index[1]

[1] Note: Page numbers followed by 'n' refer to notes.

© The Author(s) 2019
J. C. Luttrell, *White People and Black Lives Matter*,
https://doi.org/10.1007/978-3-030-22489-9

135